MANAGING TO SERVE

Learning from Catering & Allied

MANAGING TO SERVE

Learning from Catering & Allied

SALLY HEAVENS and JOHN CHILD
with
MARC VERSTRINGHE

RH BUSINESS BOOKS
Cambridge
2002

First Published November 2002

British Library Cataloguing-in-Publication Data
A Catalogue record for this book is available from
the British Library

ISBN 1 900592 38 X

Published by RH Business Books
2, Lowfields, Little Eversden, Cambridge, CB3 7HJ

Printed by E. & E. Plumridge Ltd.,
Linton, Cambridge, England

CONTENTS

Chapters

LIST OF ILLUSTRATIONS

Centre Illustrations (between pp 82 and 83)

1. A restaurant at work

2. Then ....

3. .... and now

4. The 5-star "canteens"
Reproduced by kind permission of the Daily Express

5. Michelin recognition 1990
Reproduced by kind permission of Michelin

6. An opinion

7. Making the difference (i)

8. Making the difference (ii)

9. West Dean College dining room
Reproduced by kind permission of West Dean College

ACKNOWLEDGEMENTS

This book would not have been possible without the time and assistance of many individuals and organizations, so generously given. The authors would like to record their particular thanks to the AMPI Trust, Nigel Anker, Bob Bacon, Sarah Banner, Ron Barwood, David Battersby, William Baxter, BHA, John Bolton, Laura Cahill, Bob Cotton, Gary Crossley, Mair Davison, Don Davenport, Mike Duffay, ECA, Derek Gardner, Vi Haire, Margaret Harrison, Garry Hawkes, HCIMA Library, Ron Hodge, John Houston, Jop Koops, Tony Mawer, Keith Moore, Jackie Osborne, Glen Owen, David Pearce, Bob Perry, Bert Pilaszek, Christos Pitelis, Roger Reeves, Mike Tremain, Martin van den Heuvel, Carole Verstringhe, Gosse Visser, Tim West, David Wood and Dan Wright.

Grateful thanks also to Berkeley Food Equipment, Cadbury Schweppes, the Daily Express, Ferro Design, Holland Catering, Michelin, PricewaterhouseCoopers, and West Dean College for kind permission to reproduce illustrative material within this book.

The authors apologise if they have inadvertently failed to acknowledge any contribution. If this should be the case, please advise the publisher so that correction can be made in any future edition.

FOREWORD

Stephen Hymer, the father-figure of the field of international business, once wrote that in (business) life practice precedes both theory and policy. It could be added that practice also informs theory and policy, often with a lag, and is itself informed by them. The present book by Sally Heavens and John Child with Marc Verstringhe is an exemplar of the interaction between those three pillars and the *primus inter pares* status of practice.

There is one way to account for particular practices, the case study approach. This book is such a case study, of an industry, a company, a team of leaders. It provides an account of contract catering, a relatively young, dynamic industry, and focuses on a leading innovative player within it, Catering & Allied. The book describes the company's history, philosophy, values and ethos, its leadership style, organization and management, its strategy and performance. In so doing, it provides a wealth of information, insight and linkages between theory, policy and practice.

In at least three cases, the practice of C&A seems to have preceded theory and policy. C&A's adoption of one of Michael Porter's generic strategies, that of focus differentiation, is one. The total commitment to customer also precedes more recent interest in customer focus. C&A's use of outsourcing predates more recent developments and discussions on the relative advantages and disadvantages of internalisation versus externalisation. C&A's philosophy of working with people, not for people, the ethos of trust between the leaders themselves, employers and employees, the company and its external contractors and strategic partners in alliances, the focus on the benefits of co-operation and mutual learning, the adoption of a 'virtual leadership' style that relies on those nearer to the action, interlink beautifully with theory and policy. Interestingly, some of C&A's policies can themselves be seen to be informed by the nature of the business and its particular circumstances; for example, customer focus informs the need for outsourcing as a means of 'growing small' and the patron-driven approach to the management of establishments.

In cases such as 'link manning', the 'combo system' and the move from satisfying needs to satisfying desires through customer surprise, it would appear that theory and policy are yet to catch up with practice. The very birth of the company's philosophy through a transfer of knowledge, skills, competences and attitudes from one industry (hotels) to another (contract catering) supports recent theory on the importance of such factors for diversification.

The authors do a very good job in blending together conceptual–policy perspectives with C&A's practice, identifying linkages and pointing to challenges for theory and policy, for example the growing internationalisation of contract catering, an inherently proximity-based activity. The authors' account also points to the role of luck, chance, and personality in shaping performance.

The authors' team itself exemplifies some of the ingredients that explain C&A's performance – specialisation, division of labour, and teamwork in a trust-based co-operative relationship, in this case between leading academics–researchers and a leading entrepreneur. The book will appeal to students, academics, entrepreneurs, managers, policy makers and the public at large.

It is a great pleasure for me to foreword this book for all the aforementioned reasons. It is particularly the case as all three authors are members of the Centre for International Business and Management (CIBAM), Cambridge University, itself a partnership between business and academia. I believe that there is much to be gained from reading this book.

Christos Pitelis
Director, CIBAM

PREFACE

At last: a management book which breaks the mould. A living, vibrant and fascinating best practice case study which brings alive the best of current management theories through a rigorous analysis of their application by one of the hospitality industry's most enterprising, innovative and congenial entrepreneurs.

Much has been written about the art and practice of management. The debate as to whether leaders are born or made continues. It is no longer sufficient to talk simply of visionary leadership in an age where transformational leadership has become the new Holy Grail.

Hot air or inspirational thought? Management gurus have been both mocked and applauded, from Sun-Tzu, the Chinese general and author of 36 strategies in 500 BC, to the management philosophers of the 20th century such as Ernest Shackleton, Peter Drucker, Warren Bennis and Henry Mintzberg through to Tom Peters, Michael Porter, Charles Handy, Gary Hamel, Sir John Harvey Jones, and Dilbert.

One thing is certain. They all agree it is human enterprise, fervent endeavour and ways of working which decide the future. And what are the ways of working that lead to individual and corporate success? Perhaps they are best summed up by Rosabeth Moss Kanter who, in one of her more 'flashing moments', described them following a lifetime of reflective observation and wisdom: the intangibles common to all enterprises that maintain 'world class' excellence are the '3 Cs' – Concepts (knowledge and ideas); Competence (the ability to operate to the highest professional standards) and Connections (the best relationships, vital for access to global resources). Omit any one and you have a recipe for disaster. This is something well captured in the competence mapping recently carried out by the Council for Excellence in Management and Leadership.

But, which concepts actually work? Which competencies are competitive drivers in a fast-changing global economy? Which connections are critical and worth investing in? In short, how do you in very practical terms create an enterprise built to last? How do you ensure your business is fit for the future? How can you build a tomorrow's company?

The answer does not necessarily lie in a requirement for more managerial texts. We do not need more facts about management. We do not need more knowledge, we need more know-how. As Anthony Jay comments in his book Management and Machiavelli, we have, over the years, amassed a great body of knowledge about corporations. There are books and libraries filled with innumerable facts, figures, speeches, studies, learned research, reports by system analysts, writing by management scientists, and texts by social psychologists. Sadly, our understanding of their meaning and application has not kept pace with our ever-growing knowledge. The more we know, the less clarity and wisdom there seems to be. As more is known, the less people seem to be able to make sense of what is going on about them. More importantly, the less we seem able to distil the drivers of what makes for increased staff satisfaction, customer satisfaction and shareholder value.

Worse still, few business leaders and entrepreneurs seem able to define the secrets of their success in a way which gives others who aspire to success the opportunity to learn from them about practical tools and techniques which will transform the ordinary into extraordinary performance.

Managing to Serve is just such a book. A rare and insightful case study which brings a fresh clarity of understanding about the drivers of business success. It does not add more to the body of knowledge about management theory but rather makes sound, practical sense of it for those seeking enlightened and continuous business improvement.

This is a 'how to' book inspired by a 'can do' man at the cutting edge of business innovation. The chapters that follow trace the lifetime experience of Marc Verstringhe, the winner of many industry awards and one of the hospitality industry's most visionary entrepreneurs with an unstoppable passion for excellence. In doing so, each chapter looks at a different cluster of ideas about management and organizational success and describes their practical application by Catering & Allied and its team, linking them to demonstrable achievements.

A recent survey by business consultants YSC of the boardrooms of the FTSE top 100 companies identified the characteristics of Britain's most successful entrepreneurs – unusual characters, driven by the need to make a difference, sufficiently confident to be different, and with the ability to simplify complex problems. Marc Verstringhe is just such an individual who, together with Kit Cuthbert, Jop Koops and a small team of people founded Catering & Allied Services (International) Ltd on 5 September 1975. Managing to Serve traces the early successes of Catering & Allied to the point 25 years later when, as a fast-growing multi-million pound operation, it had the highest level of staff productivity of any contract caterer.

In this book, Sally Heavens and John Child, with Marc, address themes such as entrepreneurship, service strategy, organization, managing partnerships and organizational boundaries, learning and knowledge management. They give an immensely valuable insight into the philosophy of management. The book also examines in some detail the competitive strategy of Catering & Allied, built around a 'total commitment to client satisfaction, no ifs or buts, by people working with us, not for us'. It draws valuable lessons from successful partenariats, mergers and acquisitions. It also captures well a vast range of ideas and insights, from managing a thousand moments of truth on one day to creating a global strategic alliance the next.

Managing to Serve is an extended case study which provides an overview of the different processes of management and organization and how these integrate into a successful business. The book provides a useful review of literature in each thematic chapter, whilst at the same time explicating the experience of the company in relation to the literature. The book will be found invaluable by MBA students and those on vocational courses. A detailed case study of one of the hospitality industry's most consistently successful companies, drawing out lessons of management best practice as it proceeds, will provide particularly appropriate reading for students in the UK, Europe and elsewhere. Equally, managers, entrepreneurs and owner-proprietors will find much of value, ideas and tips for success which they can take on board in their own operations.

Tourism and hospitality is a fast-growing industry sector, employing 8% of the UK workforce. Over the past ten years it has created one in five of all new jobs and contributes over £75bn each year to the UK economy. Over the next five years, it is set to create an additional 300,000 jobs. Never before has the need for enterprising ideas and entrepreneurial skills been more acute. Managing to Serve is a book come of its time. It provides a blueprint for those who seek successfully to create and sustain a thriving, vibrant and competitive tourism and hospitality business in the 21st century.

It is a book for industry giants and start-ups alike. The book offers stimulation and help to see problems in a new light. It is not a management textbook; it is about work and how it can be changed for the better. Based on the practical experiences of Catering & Allied, it is very much about delivering total client satisfaction whilst improving the lives of the people working within the organization, and making money for its investors, in a more humane yet exhilarating way. This landmark book is very much a tribute to the core values of Catering & Allied and its achievements which for over 25 years have centred on not changing what is, but creating what is not.

I commend this book to you.

David L N Battersby OBE MSc FRSA
Managing Director
Hospitality and Leisure Manpower

Chapter One

Contract catering: An overview

Looking at the multi billion pound turnover of UK based contract catering organizations today and their increasingly global perspective, it is fascinating to consider the shared history of major companies such as Compass, Gardner Merchant (latterly Sodexho) and Granada in industrial canteens. This chapter discusses the evolution and growth of contract catering, market segments and diversification of service provision within the industry, main UK players and competitive strategy. In so doing, it seeks to create a context in which the experiences of Catering and Allied International Services, on which this book is based, may be more clearly understood.

Contract catering lies within the food management sector of the catering industry, first defined by the British Hotels, Restaurants and Caterers Association (BHRCA) in their original survey of an industry 'notoriously badly served with statistics'. The BHRCA *Contract Catering Survey 1990* was compiled from source data elicited from 25 national contract catering companies and defines food management as 'the sector where the provision of meals is not the main activity of the outlet'. There are two principal methods of such provision: by means of catering staff directly employed by the organization (self-operated) or by means of a catering contractor (contracted out). Over the past decade, the range of non-catering services offered by contract caterers has broadened (i.e. workplace retailing, cleaning, domestic management and security services) but the core definition remains the same: feeding people at work.

As an industry, however, contract catering is still relatively new. Year on year growth has been annually tracked by the BHRCA - which in 1992 changed to the British Hospitality Association (BHA) - since their original survey of 1990. This reported a total of 8,780 contract catering outlets in the operating year ended 1989, comprising industry and commerce (within which segment the activities of Catering & Allied are located), education, local authority, Ministry of Defence, and 'other' (i.e. oil rigs, training centres, construction sites, and public catering) sectors. Of these, industry and commerce accounted for 81%, i.e.

1

7,089, of the total contract catering outlets, serving 63%, i.e. 304.4m, meals of the total 484m supplied. In a wider context, the total number of meals provided by self operators and contract caterers within the sector of industry and commerce amounted to 596.9m through 22,500 outlets, giving contract caterers a 51% share of meals through 31.5% of the total outlets in this sector. (NB: In the BHA *Contract Catering Survey 2000*, the definition of contract catering outlet is given as: 'any catering unit (or part of catering unit) which is separately operated and managed; a catering unit could have a number of different outlets'.)

The total UK turnover of the contract catering market amounted to £977m, or 7.9% of the overall UK catering market turnover of £12.3bn. Operations overseas were simply referred to in terms of the 14 countries operated in by UK contractors. By the time of the BHA *Contract Catering Survey 1993*, however, note could be made that the turnover of overseas operations of contract catering companies registered and based in the UK had more than doubled during the operating year ended 1992, from £125m to £277m. The bulk of this increase had resulted from expansion in EC countries, with the observation that 'overseas turnover is not included in the UK figures but it is noticeable that earnings from overseas, at 17%, is becoming a more significant proportion of the UK contract catering industry's total earnings'.

The BHA *Contract Catering Survey 2002*, relating to the operating year ended 2001, reports UK turnover in the industry rising to £3.514bn, an increase of 16.7% on the figure for 1999 when 'the £3bn level was breached for the first time' (BHA *Contract Catering Survey 2000*). The total number of UK outlets operated by contractors was 18,513, with the business and industry segment accounting for 48.6% of this figure, i.e. 9002 outlets.

A comparison of figures over a ten year period (cf BHRCA 1990 and BHA 2000 surveys) yields two points of particular note: i) the number of business and industry outlets within the contract catering market expressed as a percentage of the total (81% in 1989, as against 49% in 1999 - which latter closely compares with the figures for 2000 and 2001) and ii) the relative value of overseas to domestic operations. Overseas turnover by UK companies in 1989 was negligible in comparison to UK turnover of £977m, whereas, just ten years later, it had outstripped the latter by upwards of £1bn. In terms of percentage increase over the previous year, whereas domestic turnover by UK based contract caterers rose by 13.5% in the operating year 1998/1999, overseas turnover leapt by over 45% in the same period.

This burgeoning globalization of contract catering, an industry that ultimately and paradoxically depends on local service delivery, raises some interesting questions for the form and nature of its continuing development and of the organizations within it. In order to gain some understanding of these growth processes and interpret the signs for the future, however, we must first return to the industry roots.

Contract catering: Background to the industry

Contract catering is clearly a dynamic industry. The fact that it is relatively young – the Key Note Market Report 1999: *Contract Catering* observes that 'contract catering has only become a major part of the UK catering scene in the last 15 years' – makes its potential even more exciting. Yet the roots that are shared through a combination of organic growth with strategic acquisitions and mergers by UK based contract caterers such as the media and hospitality group Granada and the worldwide food service organization Compass (which announced their own coming together in May 2000), Gardner Merchant (which entered a strategic alliance with the French firm Sodexho in 1995 and eventually adopted the Sodexho name in February 2000) and Catering & Allied (whose partnership with the French company Elior dates from 1995), reach far back into British social history. The increasingly global perspective and cosmopolitan culture of UK based contract catering organizations today throws their origins into fascinating relief and yet, however the industry may grow, and change, and globalize, certain premises remain constant and may be seen to underpin the whole. The following observation, made by Dr K G Fenelon, then director of the Department of Industrial Administration, Manchester College of Technology, concerned industrial canteens in World War II Britain but is equally applicable today, in that it addresses basic, unchanging human needs:

3

A canteen must be something more than a mere eating place. Rest and change are equally necessary if a maximum of efficiency is to be attained. Restful, pleasant canteens for workers provide a very useful antidote to physical, mental, and nervous strain. There should be a social atmosphere which will foster good will and tolerance between workers. It can be invaluable in improving relations between the workers themselves.

(Caterer & Hotelkeeper, 31 January 1941)

The concept of feeding staff at work did not originate in the last war, however; as Heller points out, the history of industrial feeding dates back to feudal times 'when the royal or baronial kitchen and dining-hall bore many similarities to a modern industrial catering unit' (1980: 12). One such similarity may be seen as the self-operation of these kitchens, as with the first factory canteens established in the 19th century. Heller notes in this regard the pioneering work of Robert Owen, whose welfare policies included kitchen and communal eating facilities for employees at his spinning works at New Lanark.

Owen has justly been seen as the father of modern industrial catering. His actions were dominated by both commercial and ethical consideration; he was convinced that his methods encouraged industry and order (1980: 15).

Other such socially enlightened 19th century firms included Cadbury, Fry, Rowntree, Lever Brothers and Colmans but, despite the growing awareness of this aspect of employee welfare, there were still only 100 or so regular factory canteens in existence at the beginning of World War I (1914-18). This number had increased to 1,000 by the end of the war, industrial catering having been recognized 'as essential for maintenance of output of munitions, particularly with regard to keeping workers happy and comfortable' (*Caterer & Hotelkeeper*, 5 December 1941).

The concept of factory canteens only really took off, however, during World War II (1939-45). This was reflected in the formation of the Industrial Catering Association (ICA), first discussed at a meeting during the Hotel, Restaurant and Catering Exhibition at Olympia in 1937 of 'men and women closely associated with many of the largest canteens in the

4

country' (*Caterer & Hotelkeeper*, 12 December 1941). The Factory (Canteens) Order 1940 introduced by Bevin, then Minister of Labour, stipulated that all factories employing 250 or more workers must provide a canteen and maintain it; wanting every war worker unable to dine at home to have a hot meal at the right time, the Ministry had for its motto "a canteen in every factory" (*Caterer and Hotelkeeper*, 10 January 1941). Thereafter, canteens proliferated; at the time of the election of the first President of the ICA, Alderman Sir Ernest Canning, in November 1941, over 100 canteens were opening each month, with 11,270 registered (*Caterer & Hotelkeeper*, 5 December 1941).

One year after VE Day (May 8, 1945), the number of industrial canteens had risen to 19,912. As noted by *Caterer & Hotelkeeper*, 5 July 1946, this figure was sustained by two main factors; firstly, the Factory (Canteens) Order 1940 was still in force, having been continued after the war as one of the provisions of the Supplies and Services (Transitional Powers) Act. There was evidence, however, that, even if the Order had been annulled, the great majority of the canteens would have been continued as they had proved their worth during the war. Secondly, although some canteens had been closed down because factories they served had ceased to function, or numbers of employees had been reduced,

> a number of new establishments (had) been set up since the war ended, mainly at small factories which were closed down or merged with others for the sake of speedier and more efficient output for the war effort but which (were) now resuming peacetime production fully on their own account.

The outlook for industrial catering was perceived to be 'bright':

> Quite apart from the effect of the Factory (Canteens) Order … Ministry of Labour inspectors, the Industrial Welfare Society and other bodies and individuals closely in touch with the industrial world report that there is little or no tendency on the part of factory owners and management to abolish facilities for feeding at the works. They have come to the conclusion that this is a sound, business proposition in addition to its purely welfare and social aspects.

> *(Caterer & Hotelkeeper, 5 July 1946)*

It is interesting to point up a financial distinction in the approaches to industrial catering provision that emerged during the war. One is embodied in the revised constitution of the ICA, published in 1941:

> To raise the standard of industrial catering generally, and to promote interchange of knowledge, of those already engaged, or about to engage, in catering in industrial organisations, institutions, stores, or offices, and such other *non-commercial catering organisations* as may be approved by the Council from time to time ... Membership of the Association shall be open to all persons holding not less than a managerial position in industrial catering, *excluding those engaged in catering activities of a profit making nature*.

> (*Caterer & Hotelkeeper*, 15 August 1941)

The other is reflected by the formation in 1942 of the National Society of Caterers to Industry (NSCI), a trade association of catering firms operating works canteens under contract with the owners. Nearly 1,000 canteens formed the initial membership, serving around 2m meals per day to industrial workers. Qualification for membership was 'the operating of a canteen in, or in the immediate vicinity of, a factory or group of factories under contract with the factory owners of managers concerned'. It was noted, however, that the Society was not concerned with the catering for commercial staffs, or for staffs of institutions (*Caterer & Hotelkeeper*, 6 February 1942).

It is instructive to note the point made by Taylor (1977: 12) concerning the apparent conflict of competitive interest that ultimately benefited the customer:

> The mixture of professional industrial catering companies and firms handling their own catering created problems for the Industrial Catering Association, but workers in factories benefited from the additional expertise.

This was the background against which firms such as Factory Canteens, founded by Jack Bateman in 1941, and Sutcliffe Catering, originally Factory Canteens (West of England), founded by John Sutcliffe in 1946, emerged and grew to play a major role in the evolution of contract catering and the organizations that dominate the industry today.

Contract catering: Major UK players

The UK contract catering industry has been dominated in recent years by three organizations: Compass, Granada and Gardner Merchant (which in February 2000 adopted the name of its French partner, Sodexho). On 17 May 2000, Compass and Granada confirmed that they were coming together in a £17.5bn merger. In figures published to support the merger (*Caterer & Hotelkeeper*, 17 May 2000; *Financial Times*, 18 May 2000), Compass showed an 8.5% increase in UK turnover to £419m in the six months ended March 2000. In terms of worldwide trading, this figure represented 15.8% of the organization's total turnover of £2.66bn in the half year ended March 2000. In respect of Granada, annual turnover of Granada Food Services had more than trebled since the company's acquisition of Sutcliffe Catering Group in 1993, from £278m to £900m in the six years to 1999 (*Caterer & Hotelkeeper*, 25 November 1999) with underlying sales growth continuing at 5% (*Caterer & Hotelkeeper*, 2 February 2000). The announced intention was for the new organization, Granada Compass, to be demerged within 12 months into two separate companies: Compass Hospitality (comprising Compass contract catering operations and Granada's hospitality division) and Granada Media. It was estimated that, within the UK, Compass Hospitality would become the market leader with about 38% of the contracted out sector (*Financial Times*, 18 May 2000).

At the time of the merger announcement, the annual projected turnover of Compass Hospitality's contract food division was £4.78bn worldwide, representing 2.8% of the estimated £169bn global food services market (self operated and contracted out) and 8.9% of the £54bn contracted out operations within it. These figures demonstrate the scope that still exists for contract catering to develop. Within the UK, for example, although the BHA *Contract Catering Survey* 2000 notes that turnover for the operating year ended 1999 breached the £3bn level for the first time, this has to be seen in the context of the total UK food services market, then calculated at £5.5bn a year (*Caterer & Hotelkeeper*, 17 May 2000). At the time, the breakdown of contracted out vs self-operated catering services was as follows:

Table 1: Global food services market

Contracted out/self-operated distribution

	Contracted Out	Self-Operated
North America	51%	49%
Europe	22%	78%
South America	18%	82%
Asia Pacific/Australasia	20%	80%

(Source: *The Financial Times*, 18 May, 2000)

This clearly represents a major impetus for international growth within the contract catering industry, for the bulk of the global food services market remains to be secured. From the perspective of Compass, the demerger from Granada took place on 2 February 2001, with subsequent press recommendation to buy shares in Compass Group (NB: *The Times*, 18 May 2000, had noted that adverse shareholder reaction to the merger announcement had wiped £2.5bn from its value overnight). Once again a standalone food service business, the key to growth for Compass was clearly identified as being the 'market for outsourcing catering facilities by companies and institutions – (an estimated) £170bn market of which only 30% is outsourced so far' (*The Sunday Telegraph*, 4 February 2001). In December 2001, the company – by now the largest foodservice organization in the world (cf Compass 2001), the increase to £8.71bn from £5.77bn the year before being ascribed to 'new contracts won and the acquisition of smaller contract caterers' – could report pre-tax profits (before exceptional items) of £583m to the year ended 30 September, on a business employing over 300,000 people in more than 90 countries (*Caterer & Hotelkeeper*, 13 December 2001).

The following two sections of this chapter consider the history of Compass and Gardner Merchant, while Chapter Two discusses that of Sutcliffe Catering, the food services group which was taken over by Granada in 1993 but is especially significant as being the company within which Marc Verstringhe developed the capabilities that ultimately led to his start up of Catering & Allied.

Gardner Merchant/Sodexho

The history of Gardner Merchant, one of the earliest UK contract caterers, exemplifies the combination of organic development with strategic mergers and acquisitions in achieving competitive growth within the industry. Itself the result of a merger in 1964, the roots of the constituent companies - John Gardner Ltd and the Lockhart Group (formed when Peter Merchant Ltd acquired Lockhart Smith in 1946) - reach back into the 19th century.

John Toulson Gardner took over his first business in 1886, a butcher's in Leadenhall Market supplying meat to clubs, banquets (including the Lord Mayor's Banquet), restaurants and chop houses within the City of London. He diversified into restaurants with the acquisition of Wilkinsons, following this with other City inn and chop house acquisitions in the years to 1920, simultaneously developing a supply organization for fish, poultry and game, coffee, cooked meats and tea to cut out the middleman. Fruit and vegetable purchasing followed, together with the acquisition of Smith and Hooey, a wine and spirit merchant, later supplemented with a cigar department. In 1916 Gardner acquired the White Swan laundry to service his growing business and, in 1918, established a Requisitions Department for the supply of crockery, glass and cutlery. Gardner's Ships' Stores Department developed from an initial provisioning of the Russian Fleet in 1904, through to provisioning the Cunard line during the heyday of leisure sea travel in the 1920s and 1930s. When he died in 1920, at the age of 62, John Gardner had built a successful, diversified retail and catering organization from nothing.

The business was carried on by Gardner's four sons, of whom the youngest, Harold, in 1929 opened the first cafeteria in the UK, following a trip to the USA. Another significant development for the company that year was its takeover of an insolvent caterer, W P Pollard. Gardner Merchant (1986: 8) notes that

> the decline of domestic service in (the 1920s) led to an increasing demand for catering services at weddings, anniversaries and coming of age parties ... Pollard ... provided the nucleus of Gardner's outdoor catering business.

The knowledge, skills and contacts brought by Pollard and a few key staff to this side of the business were significant factors in its successful development from the 1930s onwards both in private and, more prominently, public outside catering; for example, Gardner's won the catering contract for the first major post-war sporting event, the Olympic Games at Wembley in 1948.

In respect of industrial catering, an initial request in 1930 for food supplies from the Ford Motor Company was followed by Gardner's first contract for an industrial canteen, at the British Legion Poppy factory. At the outbreak of World War II in 1939, the company was running about 30 canteens; by the time war ended, six years later, this number had increased to 600. Client satisfaction and networking were clearly significant elements in business growth; the first issue of the house newspaper, the J G Gazette, published in August 1946 carried a charming description of the 'perfect' area manager, a 'fabulous creature', that still resonates with its insights into management issues:

> For instance, while explaining to the baker that the best pastry does not contain bits of string, he must also know why there is no soup on the menu of a canteen twenty miles away. This uncanny gift of second sight also allows him to ... be able to explain to the Canteen Committee, the local Railway Official and his London office why it was that Fireman Bloggs was refused spam and chips at 1.45am on the morning of the 21st ... He is a man's man, a ladies' man, a model husband, a father, a good caterer, a fast dealer, a technical expert, a purchasing agent and a magician. He must attend meetings, marriages and funerals, ... visit customers in hospital and gaol, contact everybody worth knowing ... and, in his spare time, look out for new business.

> (*Gardner Merchant*, 1986: 17)

In relation to its other activities, industrial catering constituted only a small part of the Gardner business in the immediate post war period, but the ten years to 1965 saw a surge in growth and diversification. The nature of industry was changing: the new canteen opened at the Max Factor plant at Bournemouth in 1960 'showed the shape of things to come' in outlets where mechanization had eased heavy labour and working hours were shorter (Gardner Merchant 1986: 19). The modern working regime was reflected in a menu that consisted of a wide selection of hot and cold snacks instead of the more traditional hot meat with vegetables, served in canteen premises designed and planned by John Gardner Ltd (a service also offered to clients by Peter Merchant). By 1961, the company was serving 1,000,000 main meals per week and 3,000,000 light meals and snacks.

The other half of Gardner Merchant originated in the late 1920s, when Herbert Merchant established a cigar business. His takeover of Barker's, a small business supplying tea and buns to building site workers, together with the development of a refreshment huts for London cab drivers, constituted Merchant's first ventures into catering. Barkers (Contractors) Ltd was introduced to establish this side of the business, obtaining contracts to cater for employees in the car factories set up in the Midlands during the 1930s.

The expansion of factories during World War II generated considerable business opportunities both for Barkers and for Practical Catering Systems Ltd, formed as a subsidiary in 1942 to provide a parallel catering service to that of Barkers but operating on the basis of a fixed annual fee. This was to become usual practice in the industry but was revolutionary in its time, the incentive being to deflect accusations of profiteering through the feeding of war workers (Gardner Merchant, 1986: 23). By the end of the war, the two companies were running 900 contracts. In 1946, Barkers Contractors changed its name to Peter Merchant Ltd and, with the decision to go public, the company directors acquired an already quoted company, Lockhart Smith, which ran a number of restaurants in the North of England (all eventually closed down following the acquisition). Lockhart Smith Ltd became the parent company of the group, developing its own supply organizations in butchery and tea.

In 1953, Practical Catering Systems offered a service to hospitals and schools. Meals provision in the latter had come into focus in 1945, when the Minister of Food, Lord Woolton, observed that 'here is much good social discipline to be learnt at the common table, and school feeding will be as great an educational benefit as it will be a material one' (Hardyment, 1995: 7).

In 1961, fearing takeover by a foreign company, the directors of the Lockhart Group approached Trust Houses Ltd. The merger of these two companies was announced in December of that year, though they continued to operate separately. Three years later, in 1964, a hostile US takeover bid likewise prompted the Gardner directors to approach Trust Houses with a view to forming a defensive alliance. Ultimately, Gardner's bought Lockhart and the enlarged company – still a subsidiary of Trust Houses – was renamed Gardner Merchant in 1967. This merger created the largest UK industrial catering group at the time.

In 1970, Trust Houses merged with Forte (Holdings) Ltd in a move described by Garry Hawkes, whose 37 year career with Gardner Merchant began with his appointment as a district supervisor for Peter Merchant in 1963 and ended with his decision to stand down as CEO of Gardner Merchant in 2000, as a 'true synergy' between Trust Houses with its hotels, Forte with its inns, teashops and in-flight catering, and Gardner Merchant with its contract catering business. In 1971, the first steps towards overseas development were taken in partnership with two South African companies, catering for industrial and mine workers. This was followed in 1972 with the company's first European business, a joint venture with Unilever.

The process of internationalization was developed and directed by Hawkes, who was appointed European MD in 1975 and moved to Holland for two years to take charge of about 60 contracts (approximately 30 in Holland, 10 in Germany and 20 in Belgium). He describes this as a cathartic experience, having gone to Europe to teach and ending up learning more than at any other point in his life. He believes he had a unique experience as a native born Briton who came to run Gardner Merchant having lived and worked in Europe and thereby experienced the consensual management style of 1960s and 1970s Europe, which was based on respect for people and a participatory approach to decision making. On being appointed MD in 1977, he returned to the UK and restructured the company into 15 regions, with the aim of creating 'a lot of little Hollands' with autonomous regions and applying his direct experience of the Dutch approach to empower and give a sense of ownership to employees. Further international expansion of the company followed under the direction of Hawkes, with entry into the US contract catering market achieved in 1979 via the purchase of a hotel business with 15 catering contracts, including the United Nations in New York. In 1977, when he became MD, Gardner Merchant had approximately 30,000 employees in four countries; by 2000, there were 60,000 employees in 30 countries.

In 1992, Hawkes led the management buyout of Gardner Merchant from Trusthouse Forte, with the involvement of 1,000 managers. At the time, the company was valued at £402m, with Forte retaining a 25% stake (Key Note, 1993). Less than three years later, in January 1995, the company was sold on for £730m to the international catering and support services company Sodexho (founded in Marseilles, France in 1966), the deal being described as an 'alliance' rather than a 'takeover' (*The Sunday Times*, 15 January 1995). Hawkes himself refers to the arrangement as being 'the honourable way out'; the only alternative countenanced was to float, but the stock market was in decline at the time. He therefore sought out a company with 'true energy' with whom to form an alliance that would be complementary to his business. Hawkes remained as CEO of Gardner Merchant until February 2000, when the company changed its name to Sodexho 'in order to benefit from the strength of this leading brand name' (Sodexho: 2000). Hawkes' strength of feeling at this was well documented at the time (cf *Caterer & Hotelkeeper*, 2 March 2000) and directly prompted his resignation from the board.

Latest trading figures from Sodexho Alliance, for the six months from 31 August 2001, show an increase in sales to £4.05bn, up from £3.68bn a year earlier, with turnover within the group's food and management services increasing by 9.9% to £3.74bn. In respect of its UK operations, turnover is up by 2.6%, with the group also reporting the gain of a number of significant contracts including a £3m contract to provide catering for more than 50,000 people at the Commonwealth Games in Manchester (*Caterer & Hotelkeeper*, 18 April 2002).

Compass

The history of Compass offers another classic example of organizational growth within the contract catering industry,

13

both organically and through mergers and acquisitions. There is also a cyclical element to the pattern in that, through the merger with Granada, the original link between two key figures in the industry was restored. Jack Bateman co-founded Factory Canteens Limited in June 1941 and was joined in 1946 by John Sutcliffe; they subsequently parted company though both continued in the contract catering industry, each growing an extremely successful business. Sutcliffe Catering was taken over in 1992 by Granada (see Chapter Two), while Bateman - who had launched The Bateman Catering Organization Limited in January 1950 - sold out in 1967 to Grand Metropolitan whose contract catering business was later renamed Compass. Thus, with the Granada Compass merger, history could be seen to be repeating itself at a distance of over 50 years, though these were now major international businesses rather than two individuals allying their expertise. It is also interesting to note that both Compass and Granada first gained entry into the contract catering market through their respective acquisitions of Bateman and Sutcliffe. Tony Mawer, who from 1962 worked closely with Jack Bateman, recalls how the deal with Grand Metropolitan came about; the MD of Golden Egg, an early retail chain of steak houses, had approached Bateman in 1967 in a bid to diversify into industrial catering but Bateman had nothing to compare the offer with. He therefore rang Sir Maxwell Joseph of Grand Metropolitan who said that, if the business were offered to him, he would give more! Thus, in September 1967, Grand Metropolitan made its first foray into industrial catering, acquiring Bateman - which by now was operating in some 300 locations across the country - for just under £1m (Compass Services 1991). This did, however, place a restriction on Bateman himself; he was obliged, as part of the deal, to stay out of the contract catering business for the next three years.

The following year, in 1968, Grand Metropolitan acquired Midland Counties Industrial Catering Limited, founded by Roland Webb on 12 June 1941 just six days after Bateman co-founded Factory Canteens. By the time of this second acquisition by Grand Metropolitan, the annual turnover of Bateman had reached £6m. Throughout the 1970s, Bateman and Midland Counties continued to compete in the market under their separate identities, although the latter was renamed

Midland Catering Limited following a board decision in 1971. By 1977, 10 years after its acquisition, Bateman annual turnover had reached £36m; by 1978, again 10 years after its acquisition, Midland Catering had gained an estimated 9% share of the contract catering market (Compass Services 1991).

In 1981, Bateman Catering and Midland Catering merged to form Grandmet Catering Services, the business being re-branded as Compass Services in 1984. Expansion continued through, *inter alia*, significant acquisitions such as that of Hamard Catering Company, which at the time of takeover in 1986 was the fourth largest contract caterer in the country with an area of operation covering Wales and the north of England. Compass UK locations had by now increased to 2,350 and the following year, in June 1987, the management buyout of Compass for £160m from Grand Metropolitan led by CEO Gerry Robinson, Charles Allen and Francis Mackay at the time represented the largest MBO ever to have taken place in the UK. Further significant developments followed including, in December 1988, the full listing of Compass Group on the London Stock Exchange, the first independent food service management company to achieve this. By the beginning of the 1990s, Compass was the brand leader in the contract catering market with a market share of approximately 35%, its position of strength consolidated by the gain of a contract with British Telecom in January 1991 that included over 500 locations and almost 3000 staff and represented, at the time, 'the largest single catering contract to be signed in Europe, with a turnover of £60m' (Compass Services 1991).

Robinson and Allen subsequently moved to Granada, with Mackay succeeding as Compass Group CEO in 1991. In 1992, the company launched a new strategy focusing on five core areas within the foodservice industry - customer and client satisfaction, market segmentation and leadership, preferred employer, operational excellence and financial performance (Compass Group Annual Report 1999) - and continued to grow its business both organically, through new sales and retention of contracts, and by further acquisitions. In respect of global expansion, several overseas companies were taken over or invested in by the Group during the period 1992-1999, significant among which were SSP (Scandinavia and airport restaurants, acquired 1993); Canteen Corporation (USA, acquired 1994); Eurest International (Europe/rest of the world, acquired 1995); Service America (USA, acquired 1996); SHRM (France, acquired 1997); DAKA International (USA, acquired 1997); and Restaurant Associates (USA, acquired 1998). 1999 saw Group investment in Selecta (Europe), P&O (Australia) and Générale Restauration (Brazil), with the merger/demerger with Granada in 2000 adding further international foodservice companies to the Group portfolio. Between 1991 and 2000, turnover leapt from £265m to £7.306bn, and total operating profit from £27m to £594m (Compass Group Annual Review 2000), a period that also saw the re-branding, in February 1996, of its business and industry foodservice operations worldwide as Eurest, the name of the French food service management company bought from Accor in July 1995. This acquisition saw Group turnover breach the £1bn level for the first time, rising to £1.436bn from £851m the year before, with the decision to adopt the name - which brought to an end Compass Services in the UK - being driven by market research showing that 'one name and one set of values ... is the best way of building ... business through international client networks' (*Caterer & Hotelkeeper*, 15 February 1996).

As earlier noted, following the Granada merger/demerger, Compass is now the largest contract caterer by turnover in the world, a position further boosted by the record breaking, 10 year contract it has recently won from the oil giant Chevron Texaco. In what is believed to be 'the biggest supply deal in the catering industry', the contract has a value up to £2.8bn and also marks the increasing move by Compass into facilities management, with provision of building maintenance, transportation and other services, thereby 'highlighting the trend of large organizations demanding a wide range of services from suppliers' (*The Times*, 14 January 2002). This point is further considered in the section below.

Contract catering – market development

Table 2 below shows the growth in UK contract catering outlets over the 10 year period ended 2001. Of particular note is the increase in healthcare outlets, and the significance of commercial contract catering (i.e. catering for the public) in context of the more traditional, non-profit making[1] outlets. It is also interesting to note that, although the total number of business and industry outlets has increased, the percentage share of the market for this sector has substantially *decreased*, from 74.7% in 1991 to 48.6% in 2001.

Table 2: Number of UK contract catering outlets 1991-2001, followed by % share of total market for year

	2001	1998	1995	1991
Business &	9002	8,410	7,574	7,775
Industry	48.6	46.3	48.5	74.7
Healthcare	960	822	397	337
	5.2	4.5	2.5	3.2
State	4,847	5,727	4,957	450
education	26.2	31.6	31.7	4.3
Independent	813	568	578	620
schools , etc	4.4	3.1	3.7	6.0
Local	543	573	451	463
authorities	2.9	3.2	2.9	4.5
Ministry	625	467	393	190
of Defence	3.4	2.6	2.5	1.8
Oil rigs,building	238	256	311	246
sites, etc	1.3	1.4	2.0	2.4
Catering for	1,485	1,328	971	324
the public	8.0	7.3	6.2	3.1
TOTAL	**18,513**	**18,151**	**15,632**	**10,405**

(Source: BHA *Contract Catering Survey* 2002)

---

[1] The BHRCA Contract Catering Survey 1990 noted that 'non-profit-making catering covers such areas as feeding people at work in industry and commerce, catering in schools, colleges and universities, hospitals and healthcare, welfare and local authorities catering, the armed services and other non-profit making outlets'.

The BHA 2002 survey also noted the broadening range of non-catering services offered by the sector, including the development of workplace retailing and the increasingly significant role of branding. At the end of the operating year 2001 there were 8,537 in-house/own branded outlets, nearly double the figure for year ended 2000 of 4,352 (BHA 2001). Support services, which cover many areas from administration/secretarial through to facilities management and reception, are also growing in significance as highlighted by the figures for the period 1995-2001; as part of a catering contract, the level has increased from 2,734 (1995) to 3,379 (2001), with an additional 1,122 support services being provided as part of a non-catering contract in 2001. This latter distinction has been statistically established for the first time in the BHA *Contract Catering Survey* 2002, although the significance of these services in shaping and driving the industry was recognized some years before:

> The catering contracting industry is continuing to move away from its catering base towards the provision of a wider range of business services. Their provision, together with the expansion and extension of new catering offers, will dictate how fast the contract catering sector continues to develop

> (BHA *Contract Catering Survey* 2000)

Two years later, the prediction is that 'future growth in some sectors will depend as much on the provision of ... ancillary services as on the provision of a catering service ... there is some belief in the industry that the provision of support services will eventually become more important than the catering provision' (BHA *Contract Catering Survey* 2002).

References

Bardsley, N (ed) (1999). *Key Note Contract Catering 1999: Market Report*. 12th Edition. Hampton: Key Note Ltd

British Hospitality Association *Contract Catering Survey 2002*

British Hospitality Association *Contract Catering Survey 2000*

British Hospitality Association *Contract Catering Survey 1993*

British Hotels, Restaurants and Caterers Association *Contract Catering Survey 1990*

Caterer & Hotelkeeper, 18 April 2002

Caterer & Hotelkeeper, 13 December 2001

Caterer & Hotelkeeper, 24 May 2000

Caterer & Hotelkeeper, 17 May 2000

Caterer & Hotelkeeper, 2 March 2000

Caterer & Hotelkeeper, 24 November 1999

Caterer & Hotelkeeper, 15 February 1996

Caterer & Hotelkeeper, 5 July 1946

Caterer & Hotelkeeper, 6 February 1942

Caterer & Hotelkeeper, 12 December 1941

Caterer & Hotelkeeper, 5 December 1941

Caterer & Hotelkeeper, 15 August 1941

Caterer & Hotelkeeper, 31 January 1941

Catering & Allied International *Senior Management Conference Proceedings*, September 1995

Compass Group *Annual Report 2001*

Compass Group *Annual Review 2000*

Compass Group *Annual Report 1999*

Compass Group *Catering for growth*, February 1999

Compass Services (UK) (1991). *Fifty years*. Private publication.

The Financial Times, 18 May 2000

Gardner Merchant (1986). *100 years of catering excellence: A history of Gardner Merchant 1886-1986*. Private publication.

Hardyment, C (1995). *Slice of life: The British way of eating since 1945*. London: BBC Books

Harrison, M. *Personal interview*, February 2000

Hawkes, G. *Personal interview*, February 2002

Heller, Robert (1980). *Food for work*. Commissioned by Sutcliffe Catering Group. Private publication

Key Note Report (1993). *Contract catering: A market sector overview*. 6th edition. Hampton: Key Note Publications

Mawer, A. *Personal interview*, October 2001

Sodexho *Corporate fact file*, March 2000

The Sunday Telegraph, 4 February 2001

The Sunday Times, 15 January 1995

Taylor, D (1977). *Fortune, fame and folly: British hotels and catering from 1878 to 1978*. Andover: Chapel River Press

The Times, 14 January 2002

The Times, 18 May 2000

Chapter Two

Catering & Allied: A Review

The aim of this book is to address, through the experiences of a specific company throughout its 25 year history, some general organizational and management principles that can be seen to inform and illuminate business strategy and structure as a whole. The wider UK based food services industry discussed in Chapter One sets the context for this case study, which focuses on the London company of Catering & Allied Services (International) whose strategy as a new business 'starting with nothing' (Verstringhe 1994) was informed by two fundamental questions: Why would clients consider Catering & Allied rather than go to the well known, established companies? And why would people want to work with Catering & Allied rather than go to these larger catering companies with their clearly defined career paths?

Catering and Allied Services (International) Limited was incorporated on 5 September 1975. The two companies within this European venture, Catering & Allied (London) and its Dutch sister Holland Catering, based in Amsterdam, opened simultaneously for business. The three founding partners, Kit Cuthbert, Jop Koops and Marc Verstringhe, were all previously with Sutcliffe Catering Group, a pioneer in international contract catering yet with roots reaching back to the industrial canteens of World War II. The principles and ethos of Sutcliffe were significant in shaping and motivating the breakaway venture, and we therefore begin with a brief study of the former up until its takeover by Stirling Guarantee Trust in 1973. This acquisition proved the catalyst for the creation of Catering & Allied; as Verstringhe recalls:

> (Stirling Guarantee Trust) wanted to make big changes immediately. One, for example, was to install centralised group services ... It quickly became a centralised bureaucracy and we learned ... how this stifles initiative ... What we also learned was the fact that when a company buys another company there is a belief that they also buy you as a person body and soul.
>
> (*Catering & Allied Services Senior Management Conference*, 1995)

Sutcliffe Catering Group

In October 1946, John Earnshaw Sutcliffe founded Factory Canteens (West of England) Ltd with a complement of just three canteens. Invalided out of the Royal Marines in 1943, he had in 1944 become managing director of Jack Bateman's company Factory Canteens (founded 1941), and part of his breakaway contract from Bateman stipulated that, in return for three canteens in the Stroud Valley, he would confine his activities to the west of England for a certain period of time. By the early 1950s, however, Sutcliffe was already well established in London and other areas, laying the foundations of the major international contract catering business that as Sutcliffe Catering Group was eventually sold in March 1993 by P&O to Granada for £360m (Key Note, 1994).

With a small number of key staff, including Squid Horton, another ex Royal Marine who joined the company in 1947 and eventually succeeded John Sutcliffe as managing director of Factory Canteens (West of England), expansion was made into Birmingham with the formation of Factory Canteens (Midlands) in 1948, followed in 1951 by the creation of Sutcliffe Catering to cover London and the surrounding area. Also in 1951, Sutcliffe's won the contract for the Port of Bristol Authority, a complex of eight canteens. Mickie O'Brien, chief instructor of a commando assault unit of the Royal Marines who had originally met John Sutcliffe in 1947 and joined his company when he left the forces four years later, was appointed to run this outlet; he recalls how he explained that he knew nothing about catering, to which Sutcliffe promptly replied: "I can't boil a .... egg"! O'Brien was eventually to become managing director of the entire Sutcliffe Catering Group. The London office opened in January 1953, once six canteens had been acquired, with Margaret Arnott (whose reminiscences, together with those of Mickie O'Brien, have been invaluable in compiling this history of the company) in charge. She was the first woman to be appointed a director of the main Sutcliffe board. Sutcliffe Northern opened in 1954, followed by Sutcliffe Wales in 1959 and an area office in Scotland in 1961. Also in 1961, Verstringhe joined the London team as an area manager, having initially been recruited as a canteen manager by the Midlands company. He succeeded Arnott as managing director of the London company in 1968, and O'Brien as group managing director of Sutcliffe Catering in 1971.

Group expansion during the 1960s continued apace, with an increasingly international thrust. During this time, John Sutcliffe bought out his co-shareholders and sold the company for £250,000 to a client, Olympia, though O'Brien notes that, except for a reporting system, the new owner 'never interfered'. He was invited with Sutcliffe to join the main board, and they extended the selling areas of the company to Amsterdam, Brussels, Dublin, Frankfurt and Sydney. The philosophy was 'to sell by having a presence on the ground to allay the fears of potential customers of management at a distance'. In 1969, Verstringhe was asked to explore the possibilities of developing Sutcliffe business in continental Europe. His research encompassed Belgium, Germany, France and The Netherlands, which latter he finally recommended as the focus for expansion. It was at this time that he was introduced to Jop Koops, a Dutch hotelier whom he subsequently recruited to the London office and who ultimately became a founding partner of Catering & Allied Services.

Sutcliffe Catering: Principles and philosophy

The history of Sutcliffe Catering is inextricably bound with that of Catering & Allied Services. The principles and practices of the former fed directly into the latter, through the personnel whose development within Sutcliffe was both facilitated by, yet simultaneously facilitated, the growth of the company. For example, innovative strategies such as link manning (see Chapter Five) and the combo system initiated by Verstringhe in 1968 (see Chapter Seven) enhanced client satisfaction, cost efficiency and staff development. These were highly successful approaches to service provision, created and developed through the integration of learning with the guiding principles of the company: high standards of catering, good liaison with the client and customers, superior staff training and, perhaps most significantly, flexibility, because *arrangements had to be made to fit with customer requirements.*

There was never any question that the service was customer led, yet success in its provision would always be predicated on staff fulfilment and a team spirit that derived in particular from the Royal Marines and was realized in highly skilled small groups combining leadership and camaraderie with the restaurateur's approach to hospitality. When Sutcliffe was acquired by Stirling Guarantee Trust, however, it appeared to Verstringhe that the new management was not so well acquainted with the special nature of the 'people aspect'. This ultimately provided the catalyst for his departure together with Cuthbert and Koops, and the creation of Catering & Allied.

> We took with us the old Sutcliffe philosophy and principles. We had ... just a few core values ... Total commitment to client satisfaction; people working with not for; creating a mentor/protégé formula of support; wanting to be amongst the best in the market place rather than the biggest; give attention to detail until it drives the bigger competitors insane; be close to your customers and your team aimed at meeting a desire rather than a need; and have fun!

> (*Catering & Allied Services Senior Management Conference*, 1995)

These were to be the guiding principles of the nascent company in 1975. They emphasise the relationship between customer and service provider, within a context of mutual fulfilment. They also foreshadow the 'continuing to grow while staying small' dilemma (Baker 1999), with the perception that company size can impact on customer relations and attention to detail. Informed by certain Sutcliffe practices, briefly discussed below, they provided a framework within which Catering & Allied could begin to develop its niche within contract catering.

Sutcliffe Catering: the organization of service provision

From an original complement of three canteens and 30 staff in 1946, Sutcliffe had by 1973 grown the business to nearly 1,000 units with just under 10,000 staff. Underpinning this growth was the philosophy, as earlier noted, to sell 'by having a presence on the ground', thereby allaying potential customer fear of management at a distance. Client contact was of paramount importance, with O'Brien further noting that, 'once your selling office has established a customer unit in virgin territory, that unit becomes your selling point'.

In order to facilitate such contact, the organization was structured on one supervisor for every ten units - each of which would have its own in-house manager - with four supervisors reporting to one area manager. In turn, four area managers would report to one director or managing director. The thinking behind this approach was that, with one supervisor to ten units, s/he could spend up to two days per month in each based on a five day working week. At one level up, an area manager with responsibility for up to 40 units would in theory be able to visit each client at least once a month, on the basis of two visits per day. At director level, with each having oversight of up to 160 units (10 x 4 x 4), it became apparent over time that numbers in excess of 100 could cause overload, resulting in the split of the larger Sutcliffe companies into, for example, Midlands and Northern.

It is interesting to compare this approach with that adopted by Catering & Allied (London), where the decision was taken early on to stay within a radius of 35 miles of head office, so that senior management could be very close to both clients and the in house team (Verstringhe, 1994).

Growing small

From the outset, Verstringhe and his co-founders were concerned to retain the core values of the company, integral to which was the continuing proximity of head office to the customer in both strategic and geographical terms. This dictated a controlled programme of expansion within a clearly identified niche market both in Holland and England, constituting a generic strategy described by Porter (1985, 1998) as 'differentiation focus'. For Catering & Allied, the provision of customized restaurant style facilities in the 1975 workplace represented an innovative departure from the generalized approach to contract catering within business and industry, anticipating by ten years a fundamental of competitive advantage as identified by Porter:

> There are two basic types of competitive advantage a firm can possess: low cost or differentiation. ... (These) lead to three generic strategies for achieving above-average performance in an industry (of which) focus strategy has two variants, cost focus and differentiation focus. ... In

differentiation focus a firm seeks differentiation in its target segment (which) must either have buyers with unusual needs or else the production and delivery system that best serves the target segment must differ from that of other industry segments. ... Such differences imply that the segments are poorly served by broadly-targeted competitors who serve them at the same time as they serve others. The focuser can thus achieve competitive advantage by dedicating itself to the segments exclusively.

(Porter, 1985, 1998: 11, 15)

The positioning of Catering & Allied as a niche player amongst its 'broadly-targeted competitors' formed the basis of its competitive strategy, its policy of 'growing small' further enabling the fundamentals of dedication and exclusivity of service. It was a philosophy that endured throughout the history of the company, as illustrated by this observation of Verstringhe in 1999:

> We don't believe in 'buying' clients. Global acquisition is already showing cracks, because clients are not given a choice. It's a matter of finding a balance between entrepreneurial flexibility and the focused planning needed for long-term growth

(Baker 1999: 29)

This perspective, with its emphasis on customer choice in an increasingly globalized/standardized environment, points up the enduring competitive advantage of a customized, client led service. As Farkas et al (1995: 25) note, 'growth can be best achieved by intimately knowing local markets and *tailoring* products ... to each one'.

Holland Catering and Catering & Allied (London) grew steadily and evenly over the years. The very first client was Akzo Chemie in Amsterdam North, followed by Bernet, Shell Moerdyk, Gist-Brocades Delft, Aldel in Delfzijl and Winterthur Insurance, all in quick succession. By the end of 1975, seven clients had been secured in The Netherlands, at which time an agreement was made with Sutcliffe Nederland not to solicit any business from one another for a period of one year. In London, the first client was Servite House, an old people's home in The

Boltons, followed by Costain the builders (five sites) and Satchwell Controls, a company in the General Electric Group. Other contracts swiftly followed, including a consultancy with Esso Petroleum. By the end of 1976, ten locations had been secured in each country, after which time the group grew, on average, by ten accounts each year. Most of them were of a significant size, as reflected in the turnover for 1999: FL 113,000,000 (£32 million) in The Netherlands and £34 million in London.

There were two main routes to acquiring new business: recommendation by existing clients and leads from staff within the company. These latter were well rewarded when they resulted in new business; an item in the London company newsletter of Autumn 1989 notes that 'the company provides substantial bonuses for sales leads – these range from £500 to £1,000 and are paid on contracts being signed'. Koops notes the particular significance of client recommendation in Holland, in an interesting comparison of the UK and Dutch markets; whereas the London company was entering a long established UK contract catering environment, the field in Holland at that time was 'wide open', with the opportunity actually to create a market in an environment in which 'a factory making frozen meals for KLM' was all that was known of the industry. Another contrast lies in his perspective on direct marketing; whilst one London MD recalls an element of cold-calling which could be effective 'depending on the homework', Koops observes that the approach of a mail-out with follow up call was tried three times in Holland with no result. The company has no marketing or PR function and has principally grown through client networking, with seven people in the field and three in the office responding to enquiries. Also significant is business retention for, as well as acquiring new business, it is, as Koops notes, of fundamental important to keep that already acquired, a philosophy that is reflected in the retention rate of >97%.

The dynamic tension created by a strategy of growth while remaining 'small' in terms of a customized, highly personalized service and attention to detail was significant in driving the company in successfully capturing its niche market. This motivating paradox was heightened by the increasing profile of

Catering & Allied within the international food services industry, as indicated by the key events in Table 1 below:

Table 1: Catering & Allied: Key events

1975 Incorporation of Catering & Allied Services (International). Sister companies Catering & Allied (London) and Holland Catering (Amsterdam) begin trading

1987 Joint venture between Catering & Allied and Justin de Blank Restaurants, headed by Digby Trout, to diversify into retail catering

1989 Industrial Catering Association (ICA) affiliates with European Catering Association (ECA) to become ECA (GB) under the chairmanship of Marc Verstringhe

1990 High Table acquired by Elior

1991 ECA affiliates with Society for Foodservice Management (SFM), USA under the presidency of Verstringhe

1992 First ECA Student of the Year Competition held in Budapest under the presidency of Verstringhe

1993 Quality Catering Partners established. Original members: Catering &Allied (UK), Holland Catering (The Netherlands), Partena (Sweden) and SV-Service (Switzerland)

1995 Creation of Eurocater: a 50/50 partnership between Elior and the three founder members of Catering & Allied

Other significant cross national partnerings: Eurest acquired by Compass; Gardner Merchant allied with Sodexho

1997 Creation of Elior Nederland through merger of Holland Catering with Elior's Dutch business, Restoplan and Le Grand Bernard, to form part of Eurocater (brand names retained)

1999 Brian Smith Catering acquired by Elior

Regrouping of Elior's UK activities; Elior stake in Eurocater now 80%

Catering & Allied joins with High Table and Elior Nederland under the Eurocater umbrella

2000 Brand names of Catering & Allied and High Table replaced by the name of Avenance

Marc Verstringhe resigns as Co-Chairman of Eurocater

Catering & Allied shareholders decide to sell their shares

Performance

With the establishment of Catering & Allied in 1975, the three founding directors were in a position to apply the core values to which they were committed. The separate identity of the new company also meant that their distinctive approach would be subjected unambiguously to the acid test of performance.

For the first 18 months of its existence, Catering & Allied and its sister company made a loss of £92,641. By the end of 1978, however, the holding company and its UK operation had moved to a profit of £12,208, with the results of Holland Catering separately showing a profit of £25,363. The group accounts were consolidated for the first time in 1979, showing a profit of £30,860, with a rise to £34,748 and an accumulated profit carried forward of £8,501 (1979, accumulated deficit £22,291) in the year ended December 1980. The company was to remain profitable for the rest of its history as an independent entity.

As Figure 2.1 indicates, between 1978 and 1982 (with a profit of £37,571 and £65,363 respectively), the level of profit grew by 74%. It dipped to £26,341 in 1983 as a result of the recession. Two years later, profit exceeded £100,000 and by 1987 it had reached over £200,000. There were two downturns in the 1990s, first when an exceptional bonus was paid to the directors on the company's 15th anniversary in 1990 and second in 1994 due to a bad debt when a major client went into liquidation. In 1995 and 1996, profits were over £1 million. A profit of £4,616,723 in 1997 was the result of the disposal of 33% of the holding in Holland Catering Specialisten to Elior Nederland with whom Catering & Allied had established a joint venture. In 1999, the whole of Catering & Allied was acquired by Eurocater, a subsidiary of the French organization Elior SA.

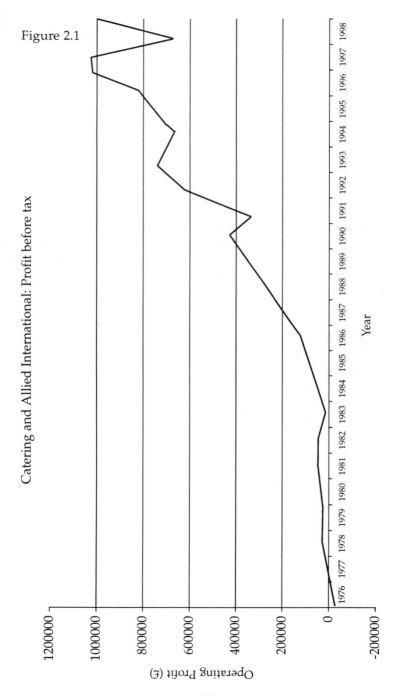

Catering and Allied International: Profit before tax

Figure 2.1

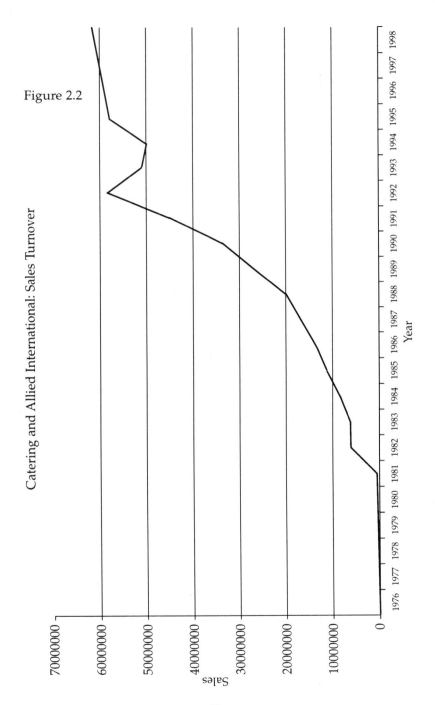

Figure 2.2

Catering and Allied International: Sales Turnover

The sales turnover achieved by Catering &Allied is shown in Figure 2.2. Until 1982, it is shown in the accounts as the management fees receivable for operating outlets. Also in the early years the turnover figures for Holland Catering in The Netherlands and Catering & Allied in the UK were published separately. This means that figures for the period 1976-1981 are not directly comparable with those of subsequent years. Thereafter, in line with the practice that had been adopted in the industry, turnover was shown as the combined figure of both the invoice charge to the clients and the turnover generated in the different restaurants. Also from that time on, the turnover for both Holland Catering Specialisten and Catering & Allied was shown in the accounts as a consolidated figure.

As shown by Figure 2.2., the company achieved consistent growth in the sales of its services until the early 1990s. In 1992, the 80% holding in Digby Trout Restaurants was acquired by Trout as part of his management buy-in., at which time DTR turnover ceased to be included in the Catering & Allied published accounts. This clearly impacted on the company sales profile. The companies' assets peaked at £2,356,478 in 1995.

Catering & Allied became extremely sound in financial terms. The original loan with which the company was established was repaid two years after its incorporation, on 1 September 1977. From that date forward, the company traded with a positive cash flow. It is estimated that the return to the original shareholders, whose funds comprised £20,000 of the initial £60,000 founding investment, was some 1600 fold.

Catering & Allied was, therefore, a company that built up a strong financial position and succeeded in achieving consistent and indeed accelerating growth over many years into the 1990s. While these achievements clearly indicate the company's sustained and successful development, however, they do not of themselves demonstrate that special performance benefits ensued from an application of its leaders' core values and the practices these led them to pioneer. For instance, we note in Chapter One the significant growth of the contract catering market in both the UK and continental Europe over the past 30 years. In a generally expanding market, the prosperity and growth of a constituent firm may signify an ability to keep abreast of competitors rather than exceptional performance.

It is possible to do more than rely on growth figures alone. There is also evidence that Catering & Allied improved its margins and outperformed its competitors in terms of productivity. One measure of a value-adding margin is the operating profit achieved by the company as a percentage of its sales turnover. It took until 1987 for this figure to reach 1%. Thereafter, except for a dip in 1990 and 1991, operating profit on sales was maintained at 1% or over, rising to a high of over 1.8% in 1995. Overall, Catering & Allied managed to improve its sales margins, which reflects a combination of efficiency and market appeal.

Other evidence shows that Catering & Allied achieved a higher level of productivity than it competitors. The following table provides information on the productivity of nine companies in 1998, calculating productivity as sales turnover divided by the number of employees.

Company	Average productivity per employee (1998) £
Catering & Allied	34,391
High Table	32,391
Sutcliffe Catering	30,711
Baxter & Platts	29,331
Compass	25,154
Sovereign	23,215
Halliday	22,185
Sodexho (Gardner Merchant)	18,290
Nelson Hind	13,249

Three companies in this list are considerably larger than the others: Compass, Sodexho and Sutcliffe Catering. They achieved an average productivity of £24,718. The figure for the smaller companies, excluding Catering & Allied, was £24,074. Catering & Allied therefore achieved 42.9% greater productivity than its peers among the smaller caterers. This is a remarkable margin of superiority, which resulted primarily from three policies discussed in later chapters: the modular management approach, the extensive use of outsourcing, and the link-manning method of restaurant management.

Outsourcing was seen by Catering & Allied's management to offer both intrinsic benefits and productivity gains. Intrinsic benefits derived from the fact that working with outside specialists allowed the company access to a greater range of expertise on a flexible basis. Thus, access to external specialists in the design of a client facility provided additional flair, added to the company's authority in the client's eyes, and generally allowed for a more flexible approach to different projects. Productivity gains arose from the reduction of costs. Outsourcing reduced the costs of on-going support services such as finance and company secretarial, PR and marketing, computing support and HRM. The following figures illustrate this cost-saving benefit (Verstringhe 1986):

Function	Outsourcing	In-house provision
Financial/secretarial	20,000	40,000
PR/Marketing	20,000	40,000
Computer Specialist	12,000	30,000
Personnel Training Dept.	12,000	30,000
	64,000	140,000

Cost Benefit

- Saving of 76,000 on income of 1,036,950
- No office space, secretary, telephone, etc.

Catering & Allied (London)

Always remembering the international context within which the company was conceived, it is interesting to consider the various approaches of Catering & Allied (London) to developing its niche in a highly competitive market. There are inevitable tensions between entrepreneurial flexibility on the one hand and strategic management and planning on the other which must be negotiated when organizing for long term growth. The potential opposition of entrepreneurship and management is discussed further in Chapter Three although it is interesting at this point to consider the following observation (italics added):

People expect good stuff. They have become used to great value for money. And they can get that from almost all companies around the world. So, being great is no longer good enough. Customer satisfaction is not enough. *To succeed we have to surprise people. We have to attract and addict them. Attention is all.*

(Ridderstråle and Nordström 2002: 278)

In other words, the perceived need in business today is to *exceed* customer expectations. It encapsulates the approach to service realized by Catering & Allied nearly 30 years ago through 'positioning (its) business to maximize the value of the capabilities that distinguish(ed) it from its competitors' (Porter 1980: 47). The following media extracts indicate the nature of its distinctive capabilities, market positioning and approach:

The workplace canteen … is being "privatised", smartened up and given a new name. … At the top end of the market are firms like Catering & Allied, who, from serving only 1.5 million meals in 1983, dished up 11.5 million in 1993. One of their smartest (staff restaurants) is at Inmarsat, a space-age communications company on London's City Road. Here, secreted in ruche-curtained alcoves, or sipping chardonnay beside an artificial lagoon, Inmarsat staff spend their lunch hour discussing the relative merits of the bream with pineapple vinaigrette as against the Pugliese bread with char-grilled vegetables and tapenade. No sign here of your traditional pie and beans …

(Middleton, 1994)

One of the selling points which Marc Verstringhe tries to stress is the "patron driven" approach. The managers put in to run a particular account are encouraged to bring their own style to the restaurant. 'We have no manuals – they restrict people' explains Kit Cuthbert. Catering believes that a proprietorial attitude fosters good standards.

(Wheatcroft, 1992)

As relative newcomers, we started out by asking: 'What have we to offer that will persuade clients to choose our service rather than other, longer established organisations operating in the same field? The answer is ... in differentiating service for similar products. ... What we did was to go back to base: to be restaurateurs first and foremost rather than administrators running a large group of canteens. In the UK we chose to specialise in staff restaurants and the boardroom within a restricted geographical area – 35 miles around London. This allowed us to stay close to the clients and close to the team on the ground. The objective is to provide a service tailored to fit each of our clients' individual requirements. The restaurants we run are our clients' restaurants: our company name would not feature on the menu; our specialist caterers would wear no company uniforms. ... We set out to ensure not only that we get the details right but that we make the whole sparkle. ... Our aim is to grow while retaining the best qualities of a small company – attention to detail, flexibility, and total commitment to client satisfaction

(Verstringhe, 1992)

Catering & Allied Chiltern

In 1989, as a direct result of the strategy to grow while staying small and informed by the patron driven approach to management, Catering & Allied Chiltern was formed to cover an area to the north west of London. With a focus of operation lying outside the original 35 mile radius of the capital, this was the first in an intended series of companies that would disseminate the ethos of ownership and independence within Catering & Allied whilst developing the business and ensuring continued client access to top management. The initiative and its outcome is described below.

Chiltern: An experiment in growth

The Chiltern initiative reflects to a great extent the influence on Verstringhe of Peters and Waterman (1982) and the attributes exhibited by 'excellent, innovative companies', with particular regard to autonomy and entrepreneurship and the 'spawning' of new, independent divisions of a business to foster

---

organizational leaders and innovators whilst remaining close to the customer base. Following discussions between the three Catering & Allied founder members on how to 'grow and stay small' (cf Sutton 1994), Chiltern was created on 1 April 1989 as a franchise experiment, a management 'buy in' concept that offered an opportunity to expand the entrepreneurial owner manager, patron driven approach into a new but related venture, in the context of a 'simultaneous loose-tight' (ibid: 15) organizational coupling. Under the terms of this arrangement, the Chiltern MD made a personal investment of 30% of the share value which, whilst reinforcing the sense of ownership, also offered the potential for capital gain in addition to salary and profit bonus through the buy back of shares by the organization at the end of the experiment – in this case, six years.

There was also a significant political factor in the creation of Chiltern, which was viewed in part by Verstringhe as a means 'to keep two good managers – Nigel Anker and London MD John Houston - in the business and stop them competing for the top job on a daily basis'. Thus the former - who had actually been brought into Catering & Allied by the latter - was offered the Chiltern venture, as MD of this satellite company that would operate outside the 35 mile limit, i.e. beyond the M25 and as far as – but not including – The Midlands, whilst remaining a member of the London board. Cuthbert was appointed as chair of the new company.

Anker describes the Catering & Allied opportunity as 'the epitome of what he had wanted to do' and the arrangement certainly appeared to work well in the beginning, as noted in the following extract from the Catering & Allied newsletter of autumn 1989 which charts the early progress of Chiltern:

'Chiltern has gained and opened three major contracts since the company's formation on 1 April. "Actually," says Nigel Anker, "we … have reached the first year's target of three new contracts within the first seven months of trading. … We want to grow slowly at the outset, winning three to four new contracts each year. By progressing in this fashion, we can continue to offer the high quality service which has enabled Catering & Allied to assume a unique position within the industry. We need to be proactive, and to offer our customers – local businesses – the same high quality, value for money service our London-based clients receive"'

(*What's Cooking*, Issue No 6)

Significant in this are the references to Catering & Allied London as a benchmark for quality, service and value for money and to the portfolio of *local* business, implicit in which is the core strategy and 'excellent attribute' of staying close to the customer.

Chiltern continued to grow over the next five years, achieving budget and returning a profit in excess of £87,000 by the end of 1994. At this time, however, as part of the process of preparing the group five year plan and financial forecasts, a review of operations indicated overhead costs for Chiltern as being disproportional to the size of the company. When coupled with the dilution to group profit by 30% in respect of private management investment, it became clear to the board of International that some action was needed to improve results. The proposal was therefore made that, whilst Anker would remain a board member of Catering & Allied London, he should now focus wholly on Chiltern with the objective of bringing the cost/profit ratio into line with the group norm.

For some time prior to this, however, Anker had privately felt that Chiltern 'was not going anywhere'. He observes that 'where it didn't quite work in principle' was that he 'couldn't get people into the system'; the route into Chiltern, which he describes as 'peripheral', was via London and it was difficult to get people - who had to have been 'senior players' in another organization - to come out again'. As a result, he felt that he was just 'one spoke of the hub, in what had been envisaged as a series of spokes', circumscribed by the wider organization.

In 1995, therefore, by mutual agreement with the London board – who by now were considering other opportunities to 'grow and stay small', principally through a partenariat agreement with the French company Elior (cf Baker 1999; Sangster 1995) - the Chiltern venture was terminated and Anker left to pursue a career in consultancy. He subsequently joined Halliday Catering

– later acquired by Wilson Storey, to form WSH - as MD and positively relates his time with Chiltern to this, noting that, without the experience gained through the venture and the opportunity to work alongside Verstringhe, he would not have gone on to 'do what he did as well as he did'. This was principally because he had the 'luxury' of a 'huge safety net' in Chiltern, which offered a unique opportunity to run an independent business without undue personal risk. From his perspective as MD of Chiltern, therefore, the whole venture was very successful, as he gained valuable experience of 'running the whole show', which he was subsequently able to apply as MD of Halliday, in a valuable translation of capabilities.

Although the Chiltern venture ultimately proved abortive, it yielded a valuable learning experience for both Anker as an individual and for Catering & Allied as a company seeking to secure its long term future. The insights it offers into wider management and organizational issues are discussed in Chapter Eight.

References

Baker, J (1999). 'Growing small'. *Caterer & Hotelkeeper*, 10 June: 28-29

Farkas, C, P de Backer and A Sheppard (1995). *Maximum leadership*. London: Orion

Harrison (née Arnott), M. *Personal interview*, February 2000

Key Note Report (1994). *Contract catering: A market sector overview*. 7th edition. Hampton: Key Note Publications

Middleton, C (1994). 'How bosses curry favour with their staff'. *Weekend Telegraph*, 8 October: 8

O'Brien, M (1992). *Personal reminiscence*. Unpublished ms

Peters, T J and R H Waterman Jr (1982). *In search of excellence*. New York: Harper & Row

Porter, M E (1985, 1998). *Competitive advantage*. New York: The Free Press

Porter, M E (1980, 1998). *Competitive strategy*. New York: The Free Press

Ridderstråle, J and K Nordström (2002). *Funky business*. 2nd edition. London: Prentice Hall

Sangster, A (1995). 'French dressing for Verstringhe'. *Caterer & Hotelkeeper*, 27 April: 7

Sutton, A (1994). 'A man who never stops learning'. *Hospitality*, April: 16-17

Verstringhe, M (1986). *A different approach to management of a people's business*. HCIMA sponsored lecture, November

Verstringhe, M (1992). 'A new approach to catering'. *First*, 6/4: 118

Verstringhe, M (1994). *Management skills into the millennium*. Paper presented at the Joint Hospitality Industry Congress, February

Verstringhe, M (1995). *Catering & Allied Services Senior Management Conference*, Castle Coombe, September

What's Cooking, Issue No 6, 1989

Wheatcroft, P (1992). 'The nosh end of the market'. *The Daily Telegraph*, 13 July: 25

Chapter Three

Entrepreneurship

In exploring the foundation and development of any business enterprise, we may usefully take for our starting point the observations of two major contributors to the literature on social and economic theory of the firm: Joseph Schumpeter and Edith Penrose. Schumpeter notes the significance of *innovation*, pointing up the dynamic tension thereby created in an evolutionary process that, as such, can only be defined in terms of its *history* and context. As such, he arrives at his theory of Creative Destruction, in which economic structures are incessantly revolutionized from within, over time:

> The fundamental impulse that sets and keeps the capitalist engine in motion comes from the new consumers' goods, the new methods of production ... the new markets, the new forms of industrial organization that capitalist enterprise creates. ... Since we are dealing with an organic process ... every piece of business strategy acquires its significance only against the background of that process and within the situation created by it. It must be seen in its role in the perennial gale of creative destruction; it cannot be understood irrespective of it or, in fact, on the hypothesis that there is a perennial lull. (1996: 83, 84)

The need is to recognize and interpret organizational behaviour "on the one hand, as a result of a piece of past history and, on the other hand, as an attempt to deal with a situation that is sure to change presently". Competition is significant in this regard; again, as seen from the perspective of innovation, where what counts is "the new commodity, the new technology, the new source of supply, the new type of organization – *competition which commands a decisive cost or quality advantage*" (1996: 84, italics added).

Implicit in the concept of competition is context. Penrose notes the context of operation, or "relevant environment" of the firm as being

> the set of opportunities for investment and growth that its entrepreneurs and managers perceive (that) is different for

41

every firm and depends on its specific collection of human and other resources. (1995: xiii)

Entrepreneurial judgment on "subjective productive opportunity" within its environment, i.e. what a firm thinks it can accomplish, thus gives rise to "expectations" that are "the immediate determinants of behaviour". The relevant environment is not, however, "an objective fact discoverable before the event", for "firms ... know (it) is not independent of their own activities" (1995: 41, 42)

We therefore see a reciprocal dynamic in the relationship between organization and environment. It is in this interaction, informed and triggered by the perception of opportunity and uniquely realized through the resources – in particular the distinctive competences - of the firm itself, that the competitive advantage of one enterprise over another may be seen to inhere.

In their study of *Decision Making at the Top* (1983), Gordon Donaldson and Jay Lorsch found that the managers of successful companies held and disseminated powerful belief systems. These beliefs were about a range of matters, including acceptable financial goals and appropriate risks, their company's distinctive competencies, where and how the company should compete, and the best ways to organize, lead and motivate staff. As Lorsch later commented,

> These beliefs, which are at the core of corporate culture, are the underlying premises that effective leaders use to shape both their strategic and organizational choices (Lorsch, 1994: 37).

Business leaders typically contribute to the evolution of their companies' belief systems over many years. It is critical for corporate success that they absorb the lessons of success and failure, and adjust their policies as the context changes. The essence of entrepreneurial leadership lies in the combined ability to articulate a clear and widely acceptable corporate culture, while at the same time retaining the flexibility to adjust it in the light of changing circumstances and the opportunities or threats these bring. This points up a significant distinction between entrepreneurship and management, with the former being expressed *inter alia* in terms of the company's distinctive competitive positioning and competence, the encouragement of innovation, a vision of how to enthuse and motivate staff and views about size and other parameters, whilst the latter tends to stress administration, control, routine and structure. These approaches are not mutually exclusive, however, and the following extracts offer some insight into the way in which entrepreneurial and management strategies cohere in achieving competitive advantage:

Catering & Allied has built its reputation on providing corporate clients with a cordon bleu-style of restaurant for employees and the ability to let the client dictate exactly how things should look and what food should be served. In none of C&A's client restaurants ... will you see a C&A logo or C&A uniforms on the catering staff. It is the ability to let the client impose his own preferences rather than apply a standard caterer's style that has enabled C&A to move very quickly in an increasingly competitive business.

(Anslow 1985)

Looking towards the 1990s the combination of good people trained and skilled with the attitude of wanting to achieve complete client satisfaction combined with using the latest technology ... is what will be required in our segment of the catering industry, i.e. catering to industry and commerce. Change is an ongoing process and what will be required in 1990 is already taking shape now – like the Dutch say – if you want flowers in the Spring one needs to plant the bulbs in the Autumn.

(Verstringhe 1988)

'To be competitive in this market, it is essential to develop and inspire people to do their best' (says Verstringhe). 'In any organization every member of staff – no matter in what position – has a point of view concerning the running of the business. Sensible management will find ways to coordinate and consider these views and bring them together, just as a conductor will draw his musicians together to perform a symphony. In doing so, the management are likely to discover changes which can be made to make the business more effective. Successful companies use a team approach, drawing at the brain power that exists at every level of the workforce, rather than only where it is institutionalized, at the top levels of management'. Not surprising, then, that a (recent independent) survey concluded that Catering and Allied Services was the company that 'most would like to work with in London'. ... On the whole, the Catering and Allied business principles are based on a flexible and innovative approach and the provision of the best-quality food in stylish environments.

(Business Magazine, July 1999)

Catering & Allied – 'An opportunity for investment and growth'

The above discussions introduce a number of factors informing and impacting on business start up and subsequent growth – entrepreneurial judgment, internal resources, business strategy, innovation, competition and environment – all of which are relevant to our consideration of Catering & Allied. The concept of strategic choice (Child 1972; 1997) is also fundamental in this regard; the courses of action decided on by the "dominant coalition" of a firm "to establish a configuration of manpower, technology, and structural arrangements which is both internally consistent and consistent with the scale and nature of operations planned". For the firm in context, strategic choice also typically includes "the manipulation of environmental features and the choice of relevant performance standards" (Child 1972), which latter factor is especially significant when considering the motivation for start up in the case of Catering & Allied.

The identification of opportunity informing the foundation of the company is given in the 'Capital requisition for the formation of a new company', prepared by Verstringhe and his colleagues, Koops and Cuthbert in March 1975, six months before their departure from Sutcliffe's. This document, fondly known as 'The Grey Book' owing to the colour of its covers, comprises a detailed analysis of group finance required, three year trading forecast, detailed budget and cash flow projections, estimated profit and loss over ten years and projected return on investment over ten years for the London and Netherlands sister companies. The motivation and objectives of the proposed group enterprise are clearly articulated:

During the past two years we have learned that our owners … do not understand our industry, its needs and its people … We are determined to save the 'spirit' of the organization that we have helped to build. The formation of our new group of companies will offer the clients a service second to none and our staff the continued 'Sutcliffe spirit' in a happy and productive working environment.

In this mission statement, we see history impacting on current context, thereby creating opportunity from the unique perspective of the entrepreneur.

The first stage of growth

In a seminal article on enterprise and business development, Churchill and Lewis (1983) construct a framework comprising five stages of company growth, beginning with 'Existence'. Of the key questions at this stage, two are especially pertinent to our discussion: "Can we get enough customers … and provide services well enough to become a viable business? Do we have enough money to cover the considerable cash demands of this start-up phase?" (1983: 32).

In other words, the need is for resources, which may be further defined as financial and non-financial. The latter category can be seen to include both tacit and explicit knowledge (Nonaka and Takeuchi 1995), core competence (Ghoshal and Bartlett 1995) and learning which, as both process and outcome, is significant for business growth through the ongoing acquisition of relevant knowledge and its realization as new competences (Child and Heavens 2001).

This perspective is informed by the concept of organizational learning as the only sustainable competitive advantage (Stata 1989), underpinning all stages of enterprise growth and development and fundamental to a knowledge-based theory of the firm (Grant 1996; Spender 1996). This theory contributes to our understanding of the strategic role of knowledge assets within a firm, and their transfer within and across organizational boundaries (Spender and Grant 1996).

When combined with entrepreneurial judgement of opportunity, knowledge as resource may be seen as the trigger for business start up and it is from this, non-financial perspective, that we first consider the resources available to the nascent Catering & Allied.

Founding the firm: From intrapreneurship to entrepreneurship

i) knowledge assets

In this section, we explore the contribution of the founder members of Catering & Allied as service providers in terms of, *inter alia*, prior history, experience, skills and knowledge, together with the network capabilities that are significant in realizing entrepreneurial opportunity (Reese and Aldrich 1995). In so doing, we illustrate the concepts of intrapreneur and entrepreneur (Macrae 1976: Pinchot 1986), which are usefully defined by Jennings et al as follows:

> Entrepreneurs appear to possess more than one talent. It follows that upon commencement of their business, they are required to be 'all things, to all men' ... They start small and learn because they have to. Not to learn is to become a minnow for the next market predator.

> Intrapreneurs, on the other hand, enter a functioning corporation. Although they may start relatively low down on the corporate ladder, the structure is already in place; there is a 'hole' for each 'peg'. Within the structure of the organization, intrapreneurs seem to possess a prudent flexibility ... (which) ... assists the intrapreneurs in their climb up the corporate ladder. (1994: 38)

Although the above serves to distinguish between two business 'types', the career of Verstringhe in particular illustrates what may be seen as the evolution of one from the other over time, through earlier intrapreneurial experience that directly informs and impacts on later entrepreneurial activity. As such, we may see the tension between history and context motivating the evolutionary process at the individual as well as organizational level.

As the son of a Belgian hotelier in the seaside resort of Knokke le Zoute, Belgium, Marc Verstringhe grew up in a business environment in which client satisfaction was of primary importance. From early on, the significance of a customized approach within the wider service context was also borne in on Verstringhe, who was encouraged by his father to become multi-lingual in order to communicate with clientele from a number of European countries including England, France, Germany and The Netherlands. The ability to converse with clients in their own language is of clear advantage in the hospitality industry but at that time, i.e. the 1930s and 40s, was a facility perhaps not so usual as it is today. Another approach of later significance lay in the organization of tasks; the hotel was small, with just 24 bedrooms so, in the interests of efficiency, nobody was assigned to a single function. Reception duties, porterage, waiting at table, serving behind the bar, cellar work and administration were all part of a normal working day. This experience directly informed the link manning approach initiated by Verstringhe at Catering & Allied.

In 1954, Verstringhe was called up for military service with the 16th CIC (Counter Intelligence Corps), attached to the 16th Armoured Division of the Belgian Forces in Germany. Being the only National Serviceman in a group of six professionals, he was taught the process of evaluating enemy strategy and tactics including the monitoring of press articles and confidential reports. Relevant knowledge acquisition, evaluation of the environment and team working were among the skills Verstringhe developed during this period that would directly inform his approach to enterprise.

Following his National Service, Verstringhe moved to England to take up the post of restaurant manager at The Lygon Arms, a 400-year-old inn in Worcestershire. He had been introduced to the proprietor, Don Russell, through friends of his father and was the first Continental European to hold this appointment with responsibility for the dining rooms and catering for banquets, weddings, and Hunt Balls. With Russell and the managing director, Douglas Barrington, as mentors, Verstringhe in particular developed his understanding of the culture and tradition of English hospitality, the customisation of service to accommodate individual preference, and a unique approach to client and staff care alike that reinforced the team concept of 'working *with*' rather than '*for*'. The association with Russell was also significant in that he was a founder member of the

Hotel and Catering Institute (HCI), later to become the HCIMA.

In 1959, after two years at the Lygon, Verstringhe took up an invitation to manage the Sywell Airport restaurant in Moulton, near Northampton. As well as this fully licensed restaurant, which had a sun terrace and lawn overlooking the airfield, Sywell Aero Club facilities included the passenger hall, which was available for private dances, dinner or meetings for up to 60 people, and a smaller assembly room with lounge and cocktail bar, together offering Verstringhe a significant opportunity to put into practice as a standalone manager all his experience to date. Amongst the changes he made were the introduction of an à la carte menu, meal of the day and fresh flowers, all of which served to enhance the reputation of the restaurant and enthuse the staff; within six months of his arrival, this previously loss making facility was trading at a profit and, as Verstringhe notes, also helping to generate a sense of community within the village, the bar and restaurant becoming regular meeting places for local farmers and business people as well as members of the Aero Club. After nine months, however, he felt the need to move on again in furtherance of his career and, in order to obviate the need for further job changes, decided to join a hotel and restaurant group within which he could develop and progress. He therefore responded to an advertisement placed by Sutcliffe Catering in national press, offering the opportunity for young people 'trained in the best hotels ... to join a catering organization whose turnover has more than doubled inside five years', beginning work with the company on 1 June 1960.

His first position was as canteen manager at GEC in Coventry, providing around 700 lunches a day with a staff of 70. Subsequently, the trade having increased to 1000 meals per day without any additional staff, he was promoted to the position of area manager within the London office. There, he met Kit Cuthbert, who was to become one of the Catering & Allied founder members, and the group managing director, Mickie O'Brien, whose leadership style was to have a lasting influence on Verstringhe especially in terms of what may seen as the encouragement of intrapreneurial activity. In 1969, a year after his appointment as managing director of the London company, Verstringhe was asked by O'Brien to explore the possibilities of developing Sutcliffe business in Continental Europe. Having carried out a survey of Belgium, Germany, France and The Netherlands, he recommended the latter. Board approval was given; O'Brien notes in his memoir that he could not have established Europe without Verstringhe, thereby illustrating the point concerning intrapreneurial specialists who must be employed 'if the company is to survive and grow in the long term' (Jennings et al 1994). A key development in Holland during this process of expansion was the introduction of Verstringhe to Jan Koops and his son, Jop. They were both hoteliers and the latter, recruited by Verstringhe to Sutcliffe's in 1969, was to become the third founder member of Catering & Allied.

In 1971, Verstringhe was appointed managing director of the entire Sutcliffe Catering group, with O'Brien as chairman. In 1973, Town and City acquired the group and lost little time in making their management presence felt; Verstringhe recalls that 'within 18 months, the conflicts of interest on how the business should proceed created a tension which became intolerable'. An ultimately creative result of the takeover, however, was the departure of Verstringhe, Cuthbert and Koops in 1975 and the foundation of Catering & Allied.

> The concept was to create two sister companies with their own names of Holland Catering and Catering & Allied London (each with) its own culture based on the culture of the country and its own financial and legal structures. In other words, the companies were not subsidiaries of a holding company but two operating companies ... with the link to Catering & Allied Services International, in order to pool resources such as know-how, experience, information technology plus legal and financial expertise, purchasing etc
>
> (Verstringhe 1999)

Integral to the venture was the knowledge and experience of Koops and Cuthbert.

As earlier noted, Jop Koops is the son of a Dutch hotelier, Jan Koops of the Hotel Amicitia in Leeuwaarden, with an upbringing very similar to Verstringhe's. His wider experience – together with proficiency in the French language - was first gained as a student during the school holidays, working at the Hotel du Nord in Charleville-Mezieres and Hotel de Paris in Monte Carlo. He studied business studies in Groningen but 'the USA was the dream' and he travelled by boat to America as a working passenger on the Holland America Line, working through 1965 at the Waldorf Astoria Hotel in New York and Market Inn in San Francisco. Following his military service in 1966-1967, in which his responsibilities as kitchen chef included catering from a mobile field kitchen for up to 4000 troops on manoeuvre, Koops became assistant manager of Restaurant Harmoni and then, in 1969, junior director at the Postiljon Heereveen. In June 1969 he joined Sutcliffe catering as a trainee manager and was instrumental with Verstringhe in the start up of Sutcliffe Nederland.

Koops describes his love for customer service and joy in working with his people as key to his philosophy of added value through partnership. For Verstringhe, he encapsulates the 'new alchemy' of Handy: 'An alchemist is a person who makes a distinctive difference to the world around him and so encourages more people to follow in their example' (Handy 1999: 13).

Kit Cuthbert, who sadly passed away on 4 December 2000, shared the background of her Catering & Allied co-founders in hotel management. Of Scottish birth, she began her career with an IMA diploma course followed by trainee management positions at the George Hotel, Edinburgh and the Hotel des Trois Rois in Basle, Switzerland. She gained further experience in hospitality as directors' cook at British Nylon Spinners, South Wales, receptionist at the George Hotel, Colchester and as manageress of the Kenco Coffee House in Chelsea before joining Sutcliffe Catering London in 1960, as an area supervisor. In 1968, she was appointed director of the company with responsibility for the West End and City business, including the implementation of the combo system (see Chapter Seven).

Koops and Verstringhe both acclaim in particular her expertise in selling, which was of critical significance in a company with no formal sales department. She was also financially astute, pointing up, for example, the disproportionate overhead costs of Chiltern (see Chapter Two). She perceived successful strategy as being rooted in teamwork and informal networking both within head office and the units, thereby enabling the contribution of ideas from personnel throughout the organization, setting great store by social interaction and general 'friendliness'. The relations subsisting between herself, Banner, Haire and Verstringhe were key, in the context of which she interrogated and challenged new ideas to their ultimate improvement, as she had done with the combo system within Sutcliffe; for example, while accepting the innovative concept of link manning within the smaller units, Haire and Verstringhe had to convince her of its viability within larger units, which they proved through altering the configuration of the team. Cuthbert was full time MD of the London company until 1983, when she became chairman. She was also board member of Eurocater, from 1995 to 2000.

Verstringhe notes the ultimate significance of trust in the relationship subsisting between Cuthbert, Koops and himself:

> We knew one another's strengths and weaknesses (and) had been successful in implementing new ideas and in growing the business. The key factor was that we had trust and believed in one another.

(Verstringhe 1999)

ii) leveraging financial resources

Having perceived a market opportunity, the onus was on Verstringhe as the leading figure in the proposed enterprise to secure the funding for start up. Section one of the business plan drawn up in March 1975 gives a breakdown of group finance required:

U.K.	Debenture	£ 60,000	To finance loss in year one of	£43,000
			At interest of 10%	£ 6,000
				£49,000
Holland	Debenture	£ 40,000	To finance loss in year one of	£29,500
			At interest of 10%	£ 4,000
				£33,500
	Total	£100,000		

On the basis of this projected requirement, Verstringhe was actively seeking potential backers from the spring of 1975. Penrose (1995: 38) notes that "successful raising of capital depends on an entrepreneur's ability to create confidence", which we may see to be effected through the social network, or role set, which begins with "a relationship or transaction between two people ... (and) consists of all those persons with whom an entrepreneur has direct relations ... partners, suppliers, customers, bankers, and family members" (Reese and Aldrich 1995). This was the approach adopted by Verstringhe.

In May 1975, at a social function organized by Olympia, the holding company of Sutcliffe, Verstringhe made first contact with the company that was ultimately to provide financial backing for Catering & Allied. He was introduced to George Gray, a director of The Halshaw Group, a Ford main dealership based in Preston. The company had already invested in a number of fast food restaurants in the north of England and was seeking to diversify. The introduction was effected by Frank Thomas who, as a supplier and friend of Verstringhe since 1966, was to become a non executive shareholding director of the new company.

By August 1975, following a series of meetings with the Halshaw board, agreement had been reached on a share issue of £20,000, split 60/40 between Catering & Allied and Halshaws. Verstringhe, Cuthbert, Koops and Thomas each had a holding of 3,000 £1 shares, with the remaining 8,000 held by the Halshaw group. Subsequently, when Halshaw sold their business to another organization, it was agreed that the Halshaw group shareholding in Catering & Allied be split between the five Halshaw directors. Two of these latter, Robert Foster and Geoffrey Smith, were to become directors of Catering & Allied although, as Verstringhe noted in a memo to his co-founders of 21 August 1975: "The important fact to be remembered is that we have 60% shareholding and are thus in control of the board". In addition to the finance raised through shares, a loan facility of £50,500 as and when required, for a maximum period of three years, was agreed by Halshaws in the form of a mortgage debenture granted on 31 March 1976. In the event, Catering & Allied called down only £10,000 of the loan and had repaid the borrowing in full by the end of August 1977, i.e. a year before it was due. Halshaws had also agreed funding of £20,000 for Holland Catering, which support was facilitated by a 'back to back' guarantee undertaken by Verstringhe's father in Belgium in an innovative move to circumvent complex exchange control regulations and the prohibitive Euro Dollar Premium.

Catering and Allied Services (International) Limited was incorporated on 5 September 1975, with Verstringhe as chairman. As noted in the company report and accounts, its principal activity was that of a holding company to sister companies carrying on business as industrial caterers (the term changed to 'contract caterers' in 1985), these being the London and Holland companies headed by Cuthbert and Koops respectively. As Chapter Two notes, after an initial 18 months of losing money, the company moved into the black, a position it never subsequently lost.

In 1983, Thomas resigned as a director and, in accordance with the Articles of Association, the three founder members had first refusal on his shares. Verstringhe, Cuthbert and Koops each purchased 1,000, thereby increasing their holding to 4,000, followed in 1984 by an even acquisition of 'B' shares. In 1985, after ten years of trading, a share conversion resulted in another holding pattern, which contrasts with the two previous years as follows:

	31.12.85		31.12.84		31.12.83	
	'A'	'B'	'A'	'B'	'A'	'B'
	of 10p each		of £1 each		of £1 each	
M Verstringhe	60000	8000	4000	534	4000	Nil
K Cuthbert	60000	8000	4000	533	4000	Nil
J Koops	60000	8000	4000	533	4000	Nil
R Foster	Nil	24000	Nil	1600	Nil	1600
W K Moore*	Nil	Nil	Nil	Nil	Nil	Nil
D Smith**	Nil	24000	Nil	1600	Nil	1600

*Appointed 6.9.84

**Appointed 21.3.79 on resignation of G Smith

In 1986, the first dividend payment was made against profits of £85,895 and an accumulated profit carried forward of £276,708. Another significant development was the approval by the Inland Revenue of the Employee Share Option Scheme; on 31 October that year, seven employees were given options to purchase 'A' ordinary shares at their current price, fixed by a payment of 10% of the value, after a period of three years had elapsed. Keith Moore, although not a direct employee of Catering & Allied, was also granted this option to subscribe for 1,000 'A' ordinary shares of 10p each at a price of 80p per share, exercisable after 31 October 1989, in what may be seen as confirmation of the strong network link forged through his provision of accounting and company secretarial services to the firm. He had been involved since the days of the business plan, having been recommended to Verstringhe by the latter's solicitor. All seven employees, together with Moore, exercised their option to purchase on 1 November 1989.

Shareholding in the group went through a further series of changes in the period to 1994, with the 'A' and 'B' ordinary shares of 10p each being converted to ordinary shares of 5p each in the year ended 31 December 1992. The accounts to the end of year 1993 show a consolidated directors' holding of ordinary shares of 5p each, as follows: M Verstringhe 522,244; K Cuthbert 522,238; J Koops 522,238; J Houston (MD London) 15,603; R Foster 154, 800; W K Moore 16,000; D Smith 154,800. In 1995, after 20 years of trading, pretax profits exceeded £1,000,000 for the first time, giving a strong basis for the 'partenariat' agreement entered into with the French company Elior in May of that year. This agreement was formalised through the creation of Eurocater Limited, a joint holding company with a 645,900 'B' ordinary share interest in Catering & Allied representing 28.8% of the share capital. Verstringhe, Koops and Cuthbert each held 16 2/3% of the issued share capital of Eurocater, i.e. a total of 50%. The directors' shareholding in Catering & Allied in the year ended 31 December 1995 was as follows:

| | 31.12.95 | | 31.12.94 |
	'A' Ordinary Shares of 5p each	'C' Ordinary Shares of 5p each	Ordinary Shares of 5p each
M Verstringhe	158,719	180,551	525,744
P Aubert*	Nil	Nil	Nil
K Cuthbert	120,825	180,551	487,238
J Koops	152,372	162,234	502,238
J Houston	63,203	Nil	72,803
R Foster	137,300	Nil	137,300
W K Moore	25,000	Nil	17,000
D Smith	137,400	Nil	137,400

*Appointed 9.5.95

The success of the group at this time is clear, and the following chapters explore in detail how innovative strategies in respect of, *inter alia*, customer relations, work organization, partnerships, learning and knowledge management all contributed to this. One factor which remained constant, however, was the philosophy of customer care which clearly informed the perception of market opportunity when the ten year business plan was originally developed in March 1975; the new company was aimed at 'the market as a whole, for companies who are in need of professional catering expertise but who want above all an economical, efficient and personalised service'.

References

Anslow, M (1985). 'Guarding the recipe'. *Your Business*, June: 35

Business Magazine (1999). 'The caring catering company'. July: 84-86

Child, J (1997). 'Strategic choice in the analysis of action, structure, organizations and environment: Retrospect and prospect'. *Organization Studies* 18/1: 43-76

Child, J (1972). 'Organizational structure, environment and performance: The role of strategic choice'. *Sociology* 6/1: 1-22

Child, J and S J Heavens (2001). 'The social constitution of organizations and its implications for organizational learning'. In M Dierkes, A B Antal, J Child and I

Nonaka (eds) *Handbook of organizational learning and knowledge*. Oxford: OUP, 308-326

Churchill, N C and V L Lewis (1983). 'The five stages of small business growth'. *Harvard Business Review* 61/3: 30-50

Donaldson, G and J W Lorsch (1983). *Decision making at the top*. New York: Basic Books

Ghoshal, S and C A Bartlett (1995). 'Changing the role of top management: Beyond structure to processes'. *Harvard Business Review* 73/1: 86-96

Grant, R M (1996). 'Toward a knowledge-based theory of the firm'. *Strategic Management Journal: Knowledge and the Firm*, 17/Special Issue: 109-122

Handy, C (1999). *The new alchemists*. London: Hutchinson

Jennings, R, C Cox and C L Cooper (1994). *Business elites: The psychology of entrepreneurs and intrapreneurs*. London: Routledge

Lorsch J W (1994). 'A decade of change for corporate leaders'. In P B Duffy (ed) *The relevance of a decade*. Boston, MA: Harvard Business School Press, 19-45

Macrae, N (1976). 'The coming entrepreneurial revolution: A survey'. *The Economist*, 261/6956/December 25: 41-65

Nonaka, I and H Takeuchi (1995). *The knowledge creating company*. Oxford: OUP

Penrose, E (1995). *The theory of the growth of the firm* (Third Edition). Oxford: OUP

Pinchot III, G (1986). *Intrapreneuring: Why you don't have to leave the corporation to become an entrepreneur*. London: Harper & Row

Reese, P R and H E Aldrich (1995). 'Entrepreneurial networks and business performance'. In S Birley and I C MacMillan (eds) *International entrepreneurship*. London: Routledge, 124-146

Schumpeter, J A (1996). *Capitalism, socialism and democracy* (Fifth Edition). London: Routledge

Spender, J-C (1996). 'Making knowledge the basis of a dynamic theory of the firm'. *Strategic Management Journal: Knowledge and the Firm*, 17/Special Issue: 45-62

Spender, J-C and R M Grant (1996). 'Knowledge and the firm: Overview'. *Strategic Management Journal: Knowledge and the Firm*, 17/Special Issue: 5-9

Stata, R (1989). 'Organizational learning – the key to management innovation'. *Sloan Management Review*, Spring, 63-74

Verstringhe, M (1988). 'The catering industry in Britain and Europe'. Paper presented at The Hotel and Catering Training Board and the Industrial Catering Association Conference, 23 November

Verstringhe, M (1999). 'Internationalisation and globalisation in the catering business'. Presentation to Deutsche Catering Kongress, Bad Homburg, 29-30 September

Chapter Four

Customer Relations: A Strategy for Service

In a business whose success depends on the identification and fulfilment of customer requirements, the philosophy of Catering & Allied – 'total commitment to client satisfaction' – can be seen both to have underpinned and informed the strategic positioning and subsequent growth of the company. Verstringhe notes the distinction between customer *need* and *desire* and, through an approach to customer service that sought to fulfil the latter within the remit of staff feeding, we understand the significance of his further distinction, as between canteens and restaurants. Perspective and terminology within industrial catering have always been critical; in considering the development of a business to which he refers as 'a minor industrial revolution' instigated by World War II, New (1957: 19) notes the barrier created by the use of the word "canteen" instead of "dining room" that

> has served in some places to put a handicap on well equipped kitchens and well furnished rooms built to serve industrial workers. The word "canteen" was too reminiscent of music hall jokes about old army canteens, stodgy foods and urn flavoured tea.

Nearly 20 years later, the opportunities created by this perception still existed; when Catering & Allied was founded in 1975 it was with the intention of 'bring(ing) some excitement to the workplace ... to create restaurants at work rather than just clinical cafeterias, canteens ... to meet a client's desire rather than a need ... for the same fee' (Verstringhe 1999). The enactment of such a philosophy would preclude any possibility of being, or doing, everything for everybody, but inherent in this deliberately selective approach was the principal marketing strategy of a company whose declared intention was to be 'restaurateurs first and foremost rather than ... administrators running large groups of canteens' (Verstringhe 1999). From the perspective of strategic growth, this decision also delimited the area of operation, restricting it to within a radius of 35 miles of head office, for implicit in a total commitment to customer satisfaction is the proximity, and accessibility, of senior management to both client and the staff who serve them.

As we see from media reports tracking the development of Catering & Allied, the ethos of customer satisfaction remained fundamental, and unchanged; the following is extracted from an interview with Verstringhe conducted in the 10th year of trading, summarizing company philosophy and service strategy:

> We always remember that we are working in somebody else's property and so it is important to involve the client in what we are doing. That's why we have no company uniform but prefer to let the client have a say in what the staff wear. It is so important to maintain a close working relationship with all our clients. By keeping our modules fairly small we are able to ensure that there is always a senior executive or director in daily touch with what is happening in every unit
>
> (*Industrial Caterer*, June/July 1985)

An early example of the client oriented, customized approach of Catering & Allied is seen in Collett Dickinson Pearce, a major advertising agency that approached the company in 1978 with a request to undertake a trial lunch in competition with another company specialising in function and boardroom catering. Catering & Allied won the contract for the restaurant designed by the agency's own architects in bistro style; highly innovative at that time for a staff feeding facility and requiring an equally attractive and creative menu. An article in the *Daily Express* reviewed this unit in 1985, seven years into the contract, interestingly invoking the concept of "canteen" to highlight the contrast between the continued widespread, deleterious perceptions of industrial catering, exacerbated at the time by media coverage of the report of the London Food Commission, and the reality of the service as provided by contractors such as Catering & Allied.

> The prawn cocktail ... was, as restaurant reviewers so succulently have it, "mouth watering". So was the Mexican liver. ... And at the ridiculously low price of £1.65, it could not be bettered. Which goes to show that not all office canteens, as the London Food Commission report

published yesterday would have us believe, are greasy, beans-and-chips-with-everything establishments. ... And what makes it even more (impressive) is that this lunch was served to me in an office canteen. In a pleasant, wine bar-style environment – fresh flowers on the table, clean table cloths, oak panelled walls – on the fifth floor of the Collett Dickinson Pearce advertising agency in London's Euston.

(Benson, 1985)

The CDP contract was an acknowledged watershed for Catering & Allied, clearly demonstrating the importance of those actually using the facility. Though benefiting from a service traditionally viewed as a welfare perquisite, with only the cost of the raw food generally being passed on to them (cf Wheatcroft 1992), staff desire has become increasingly important for, as Koops observes: 'if the eating customer is not satisfied, you're out'. Within contract catering, therefore, we can identify two distinct customer groups: the client organization within whose premises the facility is housed and for whom, as noted by Vi Haire, Catering & Allied operations director for over 20 years, the fundamental issue is budgetary; and the eating customer, who has become increasingly discriminating and whose priorities are those of any restaurant or café aficionado. As Mennell notes (1985: 20):

When people are sure of enough to eat, 'taste' is important. Taste, in food as in other domains of culture, implies discrimination, standards of good and bad, the acceptance of some things and the rejection of others. Good cooking revives the jaded appetite.

Not only does good cooking revive, it can also educate; Catering & Allied was a pioneer in campaigning for healthy eating at work, initiating in the autumn of 1985 a seminar series entitled 'Hungry for Health':

(the) seminars are held monthly, led by .. a consultant nutritionist, to enable unit managers and staff from each site to achieve a better understanding of nutrition and balancing the diet. Vegetarian dishes have been available as a regular feature of Catering & Allied's menus for quite some time and it is estimated that around 10 per cent of customers no longer eat meat or fish. ... The director responsible for the planning of a programme to encourage the use of high quality natural foods as ingredients in nourishing and attractive dishes is Vi Haire who ... said: 'We try not to overwhelm people with the health idea but instead make the food attractive and interesting. If we made healthy foods obligatory, then people would not go for it. Most customers feel well on good food but on the other hand we would never stop people from eating chips because, if we did, they would just go elsewhere'. The emphasis is fairly and squarely on education offering an alternative.

Office Equipment Index, April 1986

Not simply meeting and exceeding (cf *SFM Report*, 1991) but *generating* expectations within both customer groups has become an increasingly challenging process, though underpinned by certain fundamentals – especially in respect of the eating clientele - that are as true today as they were in the immediate post-war period:

> ... every member of a canteen staff looks, or should look, on the job not as just feeding workers in a canteen, but as a skilled trade which attracts not only the eye but the appetite as well. The standard of meals should not be measured only by their nutritional value. The customer entering a works dining-room must feel that he is in a good type restaurant, where he will obtain a meal served by a staff pleased to see him. Not only must the staff convey this sense, but the manager ... should have that personality that makes a good host as well as a good administrator.

(New 1957: 19)

Several elements are thus synthesized in the management of such a service, with customer relations key among them; the manager as host as well as administrator. This patron driven approach is fundamental within Catering & Allied, realizing the key considerations of people, food and environment (*Industrial Caterer*, 1985) that underpin the company philosophy of total commitment to client satisfaction. In commenting on the increasingly tough competition amongst contract caterers, Wheatcroft (1992) observes:

One of the selling points which Marc Verstringhe tries to stress is the "patron driven" approach favoured by Catering. The managers put in to run a particular account are encouraged to bring their own style to the restaurant. ... Catering believes that a proprietorial attitude fosters good standards.

Implicit in this approach is a close client/contractor interaction that, co-existing with the restaurant host/customer dynamic, creates a key strategic position in which the unit manager can be seen to mediate a unique relationship between staff as eating clientele and employer as facility provider. Issues of communication, trust and information 'gatekeeping' (cf Pettigrew 1973) are fundamental in this regard. The patron-driven style of unit management is also significant in terms of personnel relations within the catering function, in an integrated role the benefits of which are summarized as follows by Verstringhe (1988):

'Patron-driven' has a distinct competitive advantage. Let's face it, customers do like to see the Patron in a restaurant and so, too, do the people who work with him. It creates a kind of ambience ... a comfortable closeness. We are determined to keep this important ingredient in our business.

(What's Cooking, 1988/4)

We have already noted in Chapter Two the way in which this need for 'comfortable closeness' impacted on the organizational structure of the company, as well as the decision to restrict operations geographically. Integral to the business plan is the innovative choreography of the hands-on restaurateur/unit manager supported by a field operator (task oriented manager), operations director and quality assurance manager in modules of no more than 20 units each. The top management team of chairman, managing director and accounts head are also directly accessible both to unit manager and client alike in the integrated support mechanism represented within Figure 4.1 below. It is interesting to consider the approach of Catering & Allied, which dates back to 1975, within the context of relationship marketing, a recently emerged concept that addresses the twin concerns of getting and keeping customers (cf Christopher et al 1991; Payne et al 1995; Peck et al 1999) and identifies the shift in business marketing from a transactional to relationship focus (cf Payne et al 1995; Dwyer and Tanner 1999). Relationship marketing results in a business becoming defined by its customer relations, with the relationship itself constituting a strategic objective (cf Fournier et al 1998; Gronroos 1995, 1996). As such, it is diametrically opposed to the transactional approach:

> transactional relationships (are) situations where buyers and sellers interact with only selfish consideration. ... (P)artnership (is) a relationship characterized by mutual commitment, high trust, and common goals.

(Dwyer and Tanner 1999: 9)

For Catering & Allied, a company with no in-house marketing or PR function, new business has consistently been attracted through the development of customer relations within this 'partnership' philosophy. The salient point, however, is that this approach was, in 1975, several years ahead of its time.

Figure 4.1. The modular management system

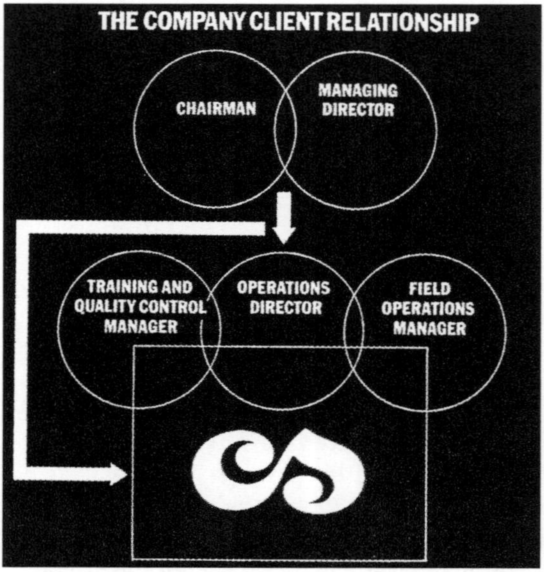

· Logo reproduced by kind permission of Cadbury Schweppes

The issue of customer relations is clearly complex, and broad based. As Hartley and Starkey (1996: 223) observe, 'customer service is … a business philosophy', in fulfilment of which are realized mutually advantageous, long-term relationships (cf Christopher et al 1991). Time is a critical factor in not simply gaining but keeping business through delivery of a customized, *exclusive* service that may be seen, paradoxically, as an *inclusive* process, integrating and creating knowledge across many levels and boundaries of client, service, and supplier organizations. Management and leadership are fundamental to the whole, and the following section considers some general theoretical perspectives on these issues and discusses their complementary role within the dynamic of customer relations. The case studies that conclude this chapter reflect *inter alia* the Catering & Allied approach to quality assurance, as key to delivery of a service by which the customer is 'no longer merely satisfied, but delighted' (Hartley and Starkey 1996: 230).

Leadership and management in customer relations

In addressing the issue of 'what leaders really do', Kotter (1999) distinguishes between the management and leadership functions, identifying a variety of features appertaining to each. These may be summarized as follows:

Management	Leadership
Planning	Setting a direction
Budgeting	Aligning people
Organizing	(e.g. the creation of coalitions to achieve
Staffing	the communicated direction/vision)
Controlling	Motivating
Problem solving	Inspiring

Although these activities are complementary, and certainly not mutually exclusive, Kotter indicates that the development of leader-managers *is* an exclusive process, taking place only at executive level: 'once a company understands the fundamental difference between leadership and management, they can begin to groom their top people to provide both' (Kotter 1999: 52). Likewise, in developing their seminal concept of leaders as 'tenants of time and context', Leavy and Wilson (1994: 6) analyse and compare 13 chief executives with particular focus on 'the challenges presented by history and context during their tenures at the top' (1994: 140). More generally, the literature has traditionally adopted a *universalist* approach to leadership through the analysis of great personalities and certain essential characteristics that can purportedly be distilled and generally applied, with, more recently, developing theories on *situational* leadership that 'attempt to identify certain leadership characteristics or behaviour that match the complexities of real life' (Heller 1996: 351). Taking the literature as a whole, however, the tendency is to reinforce the view of leader as organizationally predominant, compounded to a certain extent by the evolving 'great company' perspective initiated by Peters and Waterman (1982) and developed by authors such as Collins and Porras who, in their analysis of the 'successful habits of visionary companies' define leadership as 'top executive(s) who displayed high levels of persistence, overcame significant obstacles, attracted dedicated people, influenced groups of people toward the achievement of goals, and played key roles in guiding their companies through crucial episodes in their history' (1998: 280).

Context is, however, relative, and it is clear that aspects of both leadership and management can exist at all levels of the organization. Originally writing in the 1920s, Mary Parker Follett noted that 'the pre-eminent leadership quality is the ability to organize all the forces there are in an enterprise and make them serve a common purpose' (Graham 1996: 168). Added to her perception that 'leadership is sometimes in one place and sometimes in another' we can understand the concept of leadership at any level in an organization and that, as a result, several leadership functions can co-exist within a company The following extract illustrates Follett's thinking on the function of any head of unit, and can usefully be applied to our understanding of service management:

> The job of the head of any unit – foreman or head of department – is to see that conditions (machines, materials, etc) are right, to see that instructions are understood, and to see that workers are trained to carry out the instructions, trained to use the methods which have been decided on as

best. The test of a foreman now is not how good he is at bossing, but how little bossing he has to do, because of the training of his men and the organization of their work

(Graham 1996: 165/6)

Within a service company such as Catering & Allied, there is the additional dimension of customer relations, where we see defining relationships developing over time from the individual unit up, through patron and team interaction with the eating customer and client organization service management, as well as from top level down, through direct and ongoing client management contact and unit team support (*see* Figure 4.1). In his analysis of service management, strategy and leadership, Normann (1991: 41) describes service systems as 'innovative linkages between human capacities', with a typical feature of service company output being 'new *social* relationships':

> ... the customer is not just an onlooker; his presence in this particular context creates a social dynamic which makes the employees conscious of their roles and their prestige, which in turn helps to create a genuine new experience and a sense of participation in the customer.

(Normann 1991: 43)

His definition of management within the service industry is 'the ability to direct social processes', with

> an important part of management consist(ing) of identifying the critical factors which make the particular service system function ... if the details do not function properly, no grand design will ever succeed. But again, since *service is a social process*, there is a need for *individual motivation and freedom*, and for freedom *at the local level* ... Many service companies enjoy tens of thousands of client contacts or *moments of truth* every day, most of them probably involving employees working in the field. There is no other way of achieving high quality in every single contact (than) by maintaining a pervasive culture and making sure that every employee not only possesses the appropriate skills but is also guided by the appropriate ethos

(Normann 1991: 44) (Italics added)

In other words, a service company is only as successful as its customer relations at grass roots level, i.e. through the realization of a social process within which *every single contact* is significant. Ethos and culture are fundamental in maintaining service quality and we have earlier discussed, in respect of Catering & Allied, the guiding principles of the founders in which all employees are nurtured. The operative word, however, is *guiding*, not *leading*, an approach that is underpinned by the organizational structure which enables staff development from restaurant upwards through the devolution of managerial responsibility within a firm support network. The following extract demonstrates, *inter alia*, the elements of planning, organizing, innovating, team building and communication that are fundamental to customer relations at restaurant level:

To make the most of the two cornerstones of catering – food and people – the company has developed a restaurant management system called Link Manning ... (with) trained staff being involved in every aspect of the catering work. And since staff enjoy the opportunity not only of preparing the food, but also of cooking it, and serving it to the customer, they take particular pride in their work. They are also happy to talk to their customers about the dishes they have prepared, with the result that a valuable cross-counter bond is established. ... daily menus are not dictated by head office, but rather each unit decides for itself what dishes to prepare. ... (The) office facilities manager at (client organization) Air Products explains: At this company we feel it is very important to look after our staff well... We spent a lot of money modifying and upgrading our counters. Now ... they allow for better food presentation and make it easy for catering staff to make contact with the customers.

Office Equipment Index, March 1984

The article from which the above is taken also points up the fact that Catering & Allied canvasses opinion within each restaurant 'to find out exactly what people to think', for 'everyone can have an opinion about food'. Such feedback is incorporated into the customized menus, with restaurant staff able to develop 'their own creative culinary flair' as well as management expertise through the innovative link manning approach (see Chapter Five). Open and ongoing communication is vital in the process, not simply in establishing and maintaining the 'cross counter bond' but also in working with client organization management, the whole process being consistently monitored and supported – *not led* - by the tripartite management team of field operations manager, operations director and quality assurance executive.

Customer relations in action: Two client perspectives

Ford Motor Company Limited

Mike Tremain, Supervisor of Food Services within Ford, has been with the company since 1966. With a background in finance, he first joined within computer operations, subsequently transferring to financial services to support the operations of the Ford catering business throughout the UK. In 1980, he moved to food services, a role in which he first became acquainted with Catering & Allied. The following, extracted from interview, points up inter alia the operation of networking and the perceptions that promoted the relationship with the company:

'My boss at the time (1987/8), Patrick Broadhurst, the manager of the financial services department, was a member of the ICA, later the ECA, and over the next two years he had some conversation with Marc Verstringhe. I became involved, and so, when we came to put some business out to tender, in late 1988/early 89, we were aware of C&A and what they were doing for people in the City. Ford was looking for that standard of catering on some of our more management staff sites. Then we actually awarded them some business that took effect from January 1990.

'What we came across with C&A was a perception of quality that we hadn't seen before with the major catering companies. That may have been because C&A put an emphasis on quality and were dealing with a client base that were prepared to put in the money to pay for that quality, whereas the other caterers, with the different client base, the contracts they were going for, were probably more cost driven and so were willing to accept a lower standard to keep the costs down.'

The correlation between quality and costings presents an interesting perspective on Catering & Allied as a niche player whose standards and expertise may be seen as both driving and delimiting factors in service provision, especially with a company such as Ford in which eating customer requirements are complex and discrete:

'When we were looking at the other, larger caterers, they were assuming we were cost driven and so they were offering us a lower standard. With C&A there wasn't a choice; being a niche player their quality, product and service was the brand and it was therefore up to us to decide. Which is why we ended up awarding C&A a small niche of our business but in the more management, more white collar sites.

'It was also perceived, and agreed by C&A, that we couldn't really put them into the more industrial, blue collar areas because they didn't have the background, the expertise in dealing with that kind of environment, i.e. the fact it's unionized, that sort of thing. So we fitted them into those sites where we felt they were best suited.'

The arrangement proved so successful that, in 1999, when Ford retendered its catering business, the Catering & Allied share was not put out. As Tremain observes, 'there's an enormous compliment there' and, at the time of interview, the company had been *in situ* for 11 years.

The client-contractor relationship clearly flourished, not least because from the very beginning it constituted a site for discussion and negotiation. This is illustrated by the following example, which also points up a significant perspective on the dual aspect of contract catering service provision and the Catering & Allied philosophy of total commitment being realized through eating customer satisfaction as *mediated* by the client. It also underscores the fact that, notwithstanding its correlation with cost, the concept of quality is ultimately context dependent; it inheres in meeting customer desire which, by its very nature, is highly personal and subjective. Tremain recalls:

'I think – and I think Marc would agree with this – in the early days, there was a bit of a learning curve within the C&A

management team in understanding and taking on the Ford business, in that they had to do things differently. For example, C&A found it difficult to appreciate the need to offer egg and chips, or baked beans, as a choice from the grill bar. Nevertheless, as it was what the customer required, and as it was a choice the customer had in the past, it was to be continued. After some initial doubts, the C&A people came round to appreciating this point of view. They realized that it wasn't detracting from the quality they were offering, but rather offering the customers a wider choice.'

Ultimately, the client-contractor relationship has realized a continuous and reciprocal learning process. The above illustrates the opportunities for learning that can derive from, in the words of Tremain, 'a bit of a culture clash in both directions' that was yet resolved 'over a period of time, very amicably'. Key in this is the reference to time, which is fundamental to the learning process, and the recognition of differences 'in both directions' that were negotiated in the context of mutual trust and respect implicit in 'very amicably'. Eleven years on, it remains a dynamic and ongoing process for, as Tremain observes, 'we both learned from the experience and we've continued to do that'.

Communications have clearly played a significant role in this, with Tremain noting the accessibility of Catering & Allied personnel as one of the strengths of the company: 'The fact that they were small in comparison to others was a strength because they could offer a very dedicated service. It was very easy to get hold of people like Marc or John Houston to take a personal interest in what we were trying to do'. The contact between Tremain and Verstringhe in particular tended to be 'more informal', being realized via 'phone calls, lunches, we just generally kept in touch with each other in terms of where we, as a client company, wanted to go, and what they were doing to achieve that'. On a more formal basis, monthly meetings for the presentation of accounts are held with the area manager looking after the Ford business, 'who for a long time was Alison Percival-Carter, and her report, i.e. Ann Cripps or Gosse Visser, plus, very occasionally, Marc or John Houston, or Dan Wright'.

This clearly illustrates the ongoing involvement of Catering & Allied with the client at all levels, from area manager through operations director to MD and chairman, although Tremain notes the particular significance of on-site personnel: 'I'm a great believer that your catering on site is very dependent on the head chef and site manager. The local area manager is also a key person; first Alison, and now Laura Cahill, both brilliant young ladies; keen, positive, impressive. I can't rate them highly enough'. It is instructive that the office of the area manager is located within Ford premises, further enabling the communication that is fundamental to customer service and client relations.

Deutsche Bank AG London

As Head of Client Services within Deutsche Bank, Glen Owen has responsibility for all 'front facing' facilities including reception, meetings rooms, audio-visual and conferencing as well as staff restaurants and fine dining. Having been in contract catering for almost 20 years, he found the transition from contractor to client 'particularly hard', but was enabled in the process by Catering & Allied whose services had first been contracted by Morgan Grenfell in 1985, some years prior to its takeover by Deutsche Bank. They were therefore well established within the bank by the time Owen came into post in 1997, though through his prior experience with Sutcliffe he had already gained the perception of Catering & Allied being 'a small company but with a very bespoke sort of set up ... everyone saw them as the quality player with very customer focused ideas'. This is interesting because, as illustrated by the following extract, the concept of quality for Owen was inextricably linked with the relationship that evolved with Ann Cripps, the operations director responsible for the contract until she left the company in 2000:

'My boss, who used to be the client contact, decided that even though I was *in situ* he would continue to deal with all catering matters and C&A could have thought that, as such, there was no need to deal with me at this time. However, Ann Cripps kept me fully in the picture; even when she was summoned in to see my predecessor without me knowing about it, she would always inform me beforehand and report back. I suppose you could say she backed the right horse, because ten months later when my boss retired it enabled me really to grow the job I was doing without anyone interfering. And the joy of it was that Ann had built up a good relationship with me because, if she hadn't, C&A would have probably also have gone very swiftly.'

This last point is particularly instructive in emphasizing the significance of good customer relations, which may ultimately prove of primary strategic importance to a service company. Service delivery, as elsewhere noted, has to be effected in 'the right way' and, from the above example, the issues inherent in this process may take precedence over other elements in the quality equation; it is the approach that is significant:

'I would say that Ann had a philosophy where she recruited and encouraged good people to come and work with her. And was adamant that she would have good people working within her team. She tried to get this spirit going of people who loved food and service and that sort of thing. And so, when I came here, there were good managers here. Ann was very, very key because she did look to employ the people and they became exceptionally important because they literally worked as a team with me and that's how it still works now.'

This encapsulates the dual Catering & Allied ethos but expressed by the service recipient, significantly expanded to incorporate people working 'with' the client as well as their company together with the dedication to food and service that is integral to 'total commitment to client satisfaction'. This capability, coupled with the strength of the client-contractor relationship, ultimately resulted in an opportunity for Catering & Allied to increase their portfolio of services to Deutsche Bank; Owen advises that:

'Basically, because they run such a good hospitality client dining service, and staff restaurants, but particularly the client dining – which consists of 13 private dining rooms with butler service, very traditional - it enabled me to persuade the bank that they would be more than capable of running reception services and meeting room services ... and it's made managing the whole of my client services department much easier and more efficient. We've got a really good team spirit now, we've got proper training going on, we've got a far more professional team ... the

C&A skills of managing staff, in other words, butlers, chefs, were translated into receptionists and meeting room support staff. So I drove it to meet my own needs, because I could see it could be done, but what it did do was show the bank that C&A had the skills, better skills, to run reception services than they could themselves, because they understand hospitality.

'I don't think they were particularly niche players in reception. In fact, I don't know if they had any other reception business but that to me was irrelevant because a receptionist greeting you as you come into the building is no different to a butler meeting you when you come into a dining room, and the manager of that area should be able to manage. I see my department running like a hotel - which is where my background started - and reception is part of a hotel. And it's the same with the company flats – they went over to C&A because, again, housekeeping, changing beds, cleaning rooms, is a hotel function.'

Apart from this increase in their portfolio of services, the company also benefited from organic growth within the bank; as Owen observes: 'Morgan Grenfell grew from 1,500 when Marc first got the contract to as it is now, 11,000, and of course they've grown with it; it's been a major client for them all the way through'. Facilities development in-house included a food court, which was one of the reasons for Owen joining the bank:

'I knew how much the bank was growing; they had all these facilities on the horizon and they really hadn't got any expertise of running them. So they needed to beef up their department with someone who was going to take on all this growth. There were plans to open up this big food court, a modern, trendy staff restaurant, and Ann had already been working on that for two years before I came on board, just general plans and talking it through. When I joined, it started to move very rapidly because we were building a new building, it needed catering services, etc, and it was interesting because she was almost briefing me on where they had got so far; and then together the two of us moved the thing forward to another dimension. It was a joint effort, really, and a complete advantage that we could build a relationship based on the fact that we had a goal for both of us to achieve.'

The food court opened in September 1999 at a cost of £3.5m, with a deli, restaurant and staff shop together with 13 new client dining rooms. The rationale was clear; as Owen observed at the time: 'We didn't want it to be a staff canteen. We wanted it to compete with the smart restaurants in the West End'. Based on 18 months of research amongst employees to discover their exact requirements, the presentation and style of food varies from à la carte in the restaurant and dining rooms to sandwiches and snacks in the deli, the latter being described by Alison Aviss, Catering & Allied operations manager for Deutsche Bank at that time, as offering 'a unique opportunity to create a fast and exciting eating concept based on current high-street trends'. An emphasis on branding and open counter displays are two examples of this influence, with the immediate success of the overall enterprise being reflected in a total gross catering turnover of £6m in its first year of operation (*Caterer & Hotelkeeper*, 8 June 2000).

The above illustrates a highly integrated client-contractor approach to *customized* business development, both facilitating and facilitated by key relations. For Owen, the main strength of Catering & Allied inhered in

'their personal attention to the individual client. They did not try and treat you as one of many ... they really wanted to get to know what makes a client tick. And understand the client's business. And that's probably where Ann was quite successful because with the changing of clients she had to report to, if she hadn't got a good idea of the culture of the organization she would have fallen completely flat because it's not just the client contact but very much that, if you don't understand the culture of that organization, you're never going to move forward. So I think they certainly here understood the culture of the organization and they give a much more personal service.'

Customer relations in action: A philosophy threatened

The following case is of particular interest in pointing up the tensions that can occur both within and between organizations when arbitrary decisions made by individuals in respect of joint projects seek to override consensus. It is also significant in illustrating the rigidity (cf Leonard Barton 1995) of the core value 'total commitment to client satisfaction' and the *total commitment to the core value itself* as demonstrated by Verstringhe and his MD.

A significant challenge to the Catering & Allied core value of total commitment to client satisfaction occurred when an important client in the city of London decided to create an additional staff restaurant in one of their offices. The client had appointed a new facilities manager with day-to-day responsibility for the project, and he decided to have the plans for the kitchen and servery (counter) layouts to be drawn up by one of his own contacts rather than by Catering & Allied.

He did, however, seek Catering & Allied approval of the plans. They found the proposed counter layout to be of a single linear design that had been superseded some 10 years previously, recommending instead a free flow system that avoids queuing and speeds up the service by around 40% as well as providing for an attractive display of food and simplifying customer choice. This recommendation was summarily dismissed, however, with the client stating that he was going to implement his method whether Catering & Allied liked it or not. Verstringhe recalls:

'From the perspective of our core value, which in this case impacted significantly on the eating customer, it was an impossible situation.

'Our MD suggested that I should accompany him to an early morning meeting with the client, under the pretence that we were *en route* to another meeting. In other words, I was *not* introduced as the founder chairman of C&A. Our client remained adamant that his proposal would be implemented, saying : "This is what I want", at which point I asked him: "Is this what you want, or what your organization wants?". This question appeared to take him by surprise, and the meeting concluded that morning with no firm decision being made.

'Afterwards, I contacted the senior client within the organization, a director of the company who had awarded us the original contract some years before and with whom I had maintained regular contact. He accepted our proposal but, in order to pacify the day-to-day client, we changed his main C&A contact who subsequently invited him to collaborate in choosing the restaurant manager. This proved positive and a good relationship developed between the two, the former believing that it was his choice of the latter that had achieved the success of the operation. There was just one condition; namely, that neither our MD nor I could go anywhere near the restaurant.

'Some six months later, however, at the request of our restaurant manager, the client invited me in. No mention at all was made about the past, nor of the fact that he was now satisfied, but over the next few months we actually secured new business through his personal recommendation of our services.

'And so we kept intact our core value; no ifs, no buts.' - just!

References

Benson, R (1985). 'The 5-star canteens'. *Daily Express*, 22 October: 9

Christopher, M, A Payne and D Ballantyne (1991). *Relationship marketing*. Oxford: Butterworth-Heinemann

Collins, J C and J I Porras (1998). *Built to last*. London: Century

Dwyer, F R and J F Tanner Jr (1999). *Business marketing: connecting strategy, relationships, and learning*. Boston: Irwin McGraw-Hill

Fournier, S, S Dobscha and D G Mick (1998). 'Preventing the premature death of relationship marketing'. *Harvard Business Review*, 76/1: 42-51

Graham, P (ed) (1996). *Mary Parker Follett: Prophet of management*. Boston, Mass: Harvard Business School Press

Gronroos, C (1996). 'Relationship marketing: Strategic and tactical implications'. *Management Decision*, 34/3: 5-14

Gronroos, C (1995). 'Relationship marketing: The strategy continuum'. *Journal of the Academy of Marketing Science* 23/4: 252-4

Hartley, B and M W Starkey (eds) (1996). *The management of sales and customer relations*. London: International Thomson Business Press

Heller, F (1997) 'Leadership', in M Warner (ed) *Concise international encyclopaedia of business and management*. London: International Thomson Business Press, 347-356

Industrial Caterer, June/July 1985

Kotter, J P (1999) *What leaders really do*. Boston, Mass: Harvard Business School Press

Leonard-Barton, D (1995). *Wellsprings of knowledge*. Boston: Harvard Business School Press

Leavy, B and D Wilson (1994). *Strategy and leadership*. London: Routledge

Mennell, S (1985). *All manners of food: eating and taste in England and France from the Middle Ages to the present*. Oxford: Basil Blackwell

New, J G (1957). *Office and works catering*. London: Business Publications

Normann, R (1991). *Service management: Strategy and leadership in service business*. Chichester: John Wiley

Office Equipment Index, April 1986

Office Equipment Index, March 1984

Payne, A, M Christopher, M Clark and H Peck (1995). *Relationship marketing for competitive advantage*. Oxford: Butterworth-Heinemann

Peck, H, A Payne, M Christopher and M Clark (1999). *Relationship marketing*. Oxford: Butterworth-Heinemann

Peter, T J and R H Waterman Jr (1982). *In search of excellence*. New York: Harper & Row

Pettigrew, A M (1973). *The politics of organizational decision-making*. London: Tavistock

Pio Kivlehan, N (2000). 'Courting success'. *Caterer & Hotelkeeper*, 8 June: 36-37

SFM Report: A publication of the Society for Foodservice Management, 'Focus '91: Exceeding customer expectations', XII/1, 1991

Verstringhe, M (1999). 'Creating new market space'. Paper presented at Catering & Allied Management Conference, Stresa, Italy, August

What's Cooking, Issue No 4, 1988

Wheatcroft, P (1992). 'The nosh end of the market'. *The Daily Telegraph*, 13 July: 25

Chapter Five

Experiments in work organization and HRM

The successful development of any business is underpinned by certain constants, significant amongst which are quality and standards. Hartley and Starkey (1996) note that responsibility for quality is that of top management alone, being one that cannot be delegated, and in the case of a new company this will come from the founding directors. Subsequent growth of the organization is, however, dependent on the personnel through whom the service or product is realized, a perspective that is pointed up by the Chief Executive of Compass Group UK, Don Davenport, in his comment on the dynamic that comes through 'having people who are as attentive as you are as an individual in quality and standards'. His observation in respect of Catering & Allied, that people and food were of equal importance in the success of the company, further emphasizes the qualitative link between personnel and product: 'top of the list, good quality food and wine, knowledge of that product, knowledge of what was the highest quality that you could do in our environment ... and people equal first, because without the people you wouldn't get it'.

HRM in the operational bloodstream

One of the key features distinguishing Human Resource Management [HRM] from more traditional Personnel Management lies in the recognition that its constituent activities have to be integrated into line or operational management. Traditional personnel management tended to be parochial, focusing on functionally distinct activities and striving to influence operational managers, often from somewhat of a psychological distance and with limited credibility. HRM, by contrast, is integrated into the role of operational managers, with a strong proactive stance and an awareness of how it should support the achievement of strategic goals (McKenna and Beech, 1995). This approach recognizes that 'managers manage people and the management of an organization's human resources is primarily a line or operating management responsibility' (Stone, 2002: 5).

It was in the 1980s that the concept of HRM began to attract attention. It reflected a move away from the traditionally adversarial climate of industrial relations towards an approach that aimed to achieve excellence in the organization through a committed and well-trained workforce. By the 1990s, the concept of human resources was receiving greater attention from business strategists who recognized that companies could secure a competitive advantage through possessing core skills and competencies that were key to meeting customer needs and could not readily be imitated by competitors. In this way, HRM was sanctified by the so-called 'resource-based view of the firm' (Barney, 1991; Mahoney and Pandian, 1992).

The practices adopted by Catering & Allied anticipated this concept of HRM by around a decade. As this chapter illustrates, the company recognized that the quality of its people was essential and integral to the quality of its service. From the start, it gave priority to training and development. It saw these, however, as being provided not just by off-the-job programmes but also, and even more significantly, from attention to designing jobs and work organization so as to provide a breadth of experience and depth of responsibility that would generate rapid and substantial learning. The company's HRM policy was grounded on innovations in the organization of its operations, notably the modular management system and link manning in a flexible approach that was also adopted in respect of HR services.

Having taken the decision to maintain a lean organizational structure, Catering & Allied had no in-house HR facility but instead operated on the basis of strategic alliance with an independent consultant. Mike Duffay, as sole proprietor of MD Personnel Services (MDPS), was retained as personnel manager of Catering & Allied from May 1988 through to November 2000, a role which grew to encompass 1400 staff over 98 locations. Interestingly, there was never a formal contract between MDPS and Catering & Allied but simply the understanding that Duffay was retained on a monthly basis, an arrangement that only came to an end when the merger with Elior yielded an internal personnel department. All managers, directors and chefs had direct access to his service, which in the early days principally constituted a telephone advisory facility with calls peaking at around 1000 a month. His remit also included, *inter alia*, running courses for managers and chefs on employment law, writing contracts and statutory paperwork, advising on letters and other documents faxed through by managers, site visits and seasonal recruitment. As an independent consultant, concurrently retained as personnel manager by a number of clients over a range of businesses, he observes that he remains 'independent of politics' with 'no pressure from that source', which is clearly an enabling factor. As employment law covers all companies, his work is not governed by a particular industry, and he has originated a number of training packages in basic and advanced employment law, controlling absenteeism, disciplinary procedures, interviewing and equal opportunities. It is, however, particularly interesting to note that the equal opportunities policy written by MDPS for Catering & Allied was commended and used as a model by the CRE for small to medium businesses.

When Catering & Allied was incorporated in 1975, the company had no contracts at all. Its founders did, however, have their reputation within Sutcliffe's to trade on; between them, Verstringhe, Cuthbert and Koops had around 40 years' experience with the firm, and the former especially had done much to develop the core competencies of the company. Appointed managing director of the London area in 1968, he created the posts of company training officer and training instructor with a view to developing craft skills in-house, as Sutcliffe's was struggling at this time to recruit sufficient personnel with craft knowledge. On succeeding to the position of group managing director in 1971, Verstringhe initiated Sutcliffe Set Standards throughout the organization as a whole, a 'wake up call beyond Watford' integral to which were the quality assurance and training standards that by this time were well established in the London business.

Key in the implementation and development of the training programme within Sutcliffe's was Sarah Banner, whose subsequent recruitment to the nascent Catering & Allied was critical in initiating, developing and sustaining the company's quality assurance and training standards. Another significant early appointment was that of Vi Haire, also from Sutcliffe's, who joined as operations manager a few weeks after Catering & Allied was founded and formed with Sarah Banner a pivotal relationship in the management system of the company. Their prior experience and competencies are discussed below, as informing two key elements of the modular approach that would become a defining feature of management structure and process within the organization.

The modular management system: Quality assurance and training

In an article published in 1988, around half way through Sarah Banner's career within Catering & Allied, she makes a number of significant points concerning the interrelationship of quality assurance and training. Catering is a creative business in which 'great emphasis (is placed) on the contribution made by the individual' yet which is underpinned by a common framework, that of quality standards and attention to detail. From her initial appointment as training officer in March 1976, Banner's role and responsibilities grew to encompass all aspects of quality assurance and training management, in a natural progression through which the 'precise nature' of quality assurance can be seen to have evolved from the training function:

> Training is, after all, about striving for improvement; it's about setting, reaching and, ideally, surpassing standards – in our case, of food preparation, counter presentation, and hygiene. It's finding out how we can motivate people on our side of the counter to work more productively as a team and it's about learning how we can motivate people on the other side of the counter, sometimes to be more adventurous in their food selection, sometimes to adapt to new technology at the point-of-sale, and occasionally to spend a little more
>
> (*What's Cooking*, June 1988)

This points up two significant facts, namely that, especially in a service industry such as catering, effective training of an *individual* takes place in a *team* environment and that integral to this process is the development of client and customer relationships. As such, there is a reciprocal learning dynamic that can mediate organizational boundaries.

The principles that were brought to bear in this approach to quality standards and training can be seen to have been nurtured within Sutcliffe's and were integral to the founding ethos of Catering & Allied. Individual flexibility, creativity and responsibility within the context of a team approach are hallmarks of the whole process, as evidenced in the career histories of key personnel such as Sarah Banner. On leaving college in 1967 with a Higher National Diploma in hotel management including 151 (advanced cheffing), she was recruited by Margaret Arnott for Sutcliffe's as boardroom chef and assistant manager within a new facility at Marconi Marine. Initially, she was 'terrified' at the responsibility, as that of the boardroom, catering for 12 directors, was hers alone and included all menu planning (typically four course lunches, with Escoffier type cuisine), food preparation and, with the assistance of two waitresses, food service and washing up. There was also a canteen for 160 general staff plus morning and afternoon trolley services offering filled rolls, cakes, tea and coffee and Banner assisted the manager of the unit with these rounds as well as the books at the end of each day. Her observation on what was clearly a formative and instructive period for her, at the very beginning of her career within the industry, is that, 'as new to the business, you had to have a go at everything *so that you understood what happened*'. There was – and is – no substitute for hands-on experience, and this 'have a go' philosophy is fundamental to the acquisition of both tacit and explicit knowledge (cf Nonaka and Takeuchi, 1995). It is, however, both time and labour intensive and requires careful planning and monitoring for a successful learning outcome as in, for example, the matching of individuals in the knowledge transfer process.

In 1968, Banner was offered the post of training instructor for Sutcliffe's London area, under the company training officer who had identified her as someone who was craft orientated, had the personality and leadership skills to undertake training, and also had a detailed knowledge of food. Both these training positions were created by Marc Verstringhe on his succession as MD of the London company that year, as it was a struggle at that time to recruit sufficient people with the requisite craft knowledge. This was because most catering college graduates went into the hotel and restaurant business, a scenario that has not altered much to this day (cf Doherty 2001). Banner recalls from her own college days that the 'canteen' business was looked down on and that students were not encouraged to go into the contract catering business at all, being told by colleges that the hotel trade was 'much better'. She, however, was 'not popular' within the hotel industry, simply because she was getting married: 'Everybody had this fear that I would produce 15 babies in 15 weeks!'

In contrast, contract catering offered her - over 30 years ago when married women were eyed askance by potential employers across many business sectors - a real opportunity for career development and progression, an interesting point when considered in the light of recent research commissioned by the Higher Education Funding Council for England on management in the hospitality industry. Salient amongst its findings is that 'the opportunities and investment in people in contract catering far outstrips (sic) that found in other sectors of hospitality' (Doherty 2001: 37). That these opportunities benefit both men and women is seen in the example of Donald Marshall, a five star hotel chef who had previously viewed contract catering as a 'step down' but in 1998 opted, at the age of 30, to work for High Table (now Avenance) because he had 'had enough of the long hours in hotels and wanted some kind of family life. In contract catering it was possible to work Monday to Friday, from 9am until 5pm.' This factor, together with the 'fantastic standards' he witnessed in many contracts, confirmed his decision to switch; he is now head chef at the Avenance facility within Lloyd's of London (*Caterer & Hotelkeeper*, 24-30 May 2001: 46).

The comment concerning standards is instructive and recalls the observation of Sarah Banner concerning the link between quality assurance and training, one that was increasingly emphasized within her role at Catering & Allied. Prior to this, her remit as training instructor within Sutcliffe's had particular regard to cheffing and an emphasis on the quality, standard and presentation of food. There were various elements to the programme with, for example, 16 year old apprentices recruited straight from school studying for their 151 (advanced cheffing) on day release and working in units the rest of the time, and

1. A restaurant at work

2. Then …

3. … and now

"It says: Canteen food can seriously damage your health. Telling that to our Florrie could seriously damage your health"

The 5-star canteens

Beware of the canteen cooks

Proof that dining at work doesn't have to be a risk

THE prawn cocktail, dressed in a home-made mayonnaise mixed with tomato purée and Worcestershire sauce, was, as restaurant reviewers so succulently it, "mouth watering." So was Mexican liver.

Firstly," explains cook Judith Henshall. ghtly sauté the liver. Then I add fresh s, fresh peppers and tomatoes."

at the ridiculously low of £1-69p, it could not be red.

ich goes to show that not lice canteens, as the London Food Commission report shed yesterday would have elieve, are greasy, beans-chips - with -every - establishments.

home, if I still had a it would have cost her at 50p more to prepare the meal

he meal you had was more tious, in terms of vitamins minerals, than most people n one meal in ten," says tionist Issy Cole-Hamilton. most impressive.

d what makes it even so is that this lunch was d to me in an office can-

In a pleasant, wine bar-environment — fresh rs on the table, clean cloths, cook panelled -on the fifth floor of the tt Dickinson Pearce rtising agency in London's on.

, everything has its price. ambiance may have been ant, the food superb, but had to be a hiccup. ngly, it was this — if I to continue eating food

By ROSS BENSON

like this, every lunchtime, day in, day out, I am quite likely to kill myself.

The problem is fat, the same fat that the London Food Commission points out, substantially increases the risk of heart disease and fatal heart attack.

🍷 **A splendid choice**

"I've worked it out," says Miss Cole-Hamilton. "Sixty four per cent of my calories in that meal came from fat— from the sautéed liver, from the mayonnaise for the prawn cocktail. And that is double what the Health Education Council recommends as the maximum intake of fat per day.

The mistake, I concede, was mine. The menu at Collett Dickinson Pearce's mock bar (not so mock—a gin and tonic

plus a half-pint of imported German beer costs only £1-15) contained a splendid choice of low fat, high fibre dishes.

Jacket potatoes, salads, homemade pea soup, brown bread sandwiches. Even the quiche is made with wholemeal flour, and there is a vegetarian ratatouille.

"People are terribly diet-conscious these days," says Vi Haire, of the caterers Catering and Allied, "so we always put a lot of high fibre on our menus."

Sorting through the menu, however, and picking out those low fat dishes isn't quite so easy — especially if one is British and brought up on a diet of baked beans, chips and meat pies.

"In the old days, when we did a lot more physical unusual work, we needed a lot more calories and fat is the cheapest way of taking these calories aboard," says Miss Cole-Hamilton.

● HOW do you rate YOUR canteen? Is it good enough to be the best in Britain? Let us know. Write to: Letters, Daily Express, Fleet Street, London, EC4P 4JT.

Now, in times of more sedentary occupations, "we don't need nearly as much fat —but we still eat it."

Eating well in staff canteens isn't quite the impossible task it used to be, however. Over at BICC, the giant cable company, I could have lunched off fresh vegetables, followed by a chicken with tarragon sauce. At the Bank of England, the canteen is said to be better than the Savoy Grill.

🍷 **A few raw vegetables**

So there was too much fat! But if I reduce myself to a piece of wholemeal bread and a few raw vegetables this evening, then no harm is done.

And besides, it was delicious. So delicious, in fact, that I am thinking of going back again tomorrow. It's Chinese Day at Collett Dickinson Pearce. . . .

Bon vivant Benson enjoying work

4. The 5-star "canteens"

Reproduced by kind permission of the Daily Express

driven operations. One company which has been set up on the crest of this particular wave is Catering & Allied, which can boast the first in-house restaurant to be mentioned in the Michelin Guide — Heal's. It

1990

XX **Heals,** First floor; Heal's Department Store, 196 Tottenham Court Rd, W1P 9LD, ✆ 636 1666 ext. 5513, Fax 631 3091 – ▤. 🛏 🝙 ⊕ 💳   KU 2
closed Sunday and Bank Holidays – M (lunch only) 25.50 £.

5. Michelin recognition 1990

Reproduced by kind permission of Michelin

total commitment because that's what I receive from Catering & Allied."

Kitch Davies

Occupation:
Chef/Manager at Designers Guild

Length of service:
Six years with Catering & Allied - the last three working at Designers Guild

Extra-curricular:
Socialising, travel, eating out, reading and music

Plans for the future:
To progress to a larger unit and take a more [...] management role.

In only six years Kitch Davies has developed from occasional kitchen work to Field Manager, responsible for recruiting managers, holiday, special projects and assisting with the opening of new contracts. It is just a typical example of how we value our people and encourage them to progress. This philosophy, of course, not only benefits them but the clients that we work with.

"Catering & Allied has a mission to give total commitment to client satisfaction - no ifs, no buts," says Kitch. "It offers a combination of the right people, right food, and as the saying goes, the real fullness."

"With clients it offers an open-minded, tailored service

to create a definition between working and eating and all our people foster this idea.

That is the way we deliver stylish, high performance catering with the ability to reflect the needs of any organisation from contemporary to traditional, upbeat to classical.

"At Designers Guild, after an initial involvement from the client, I gained the freedom to influence the menu as the relationship developed", points out Kitch. "Both they and Catering & Allied allowed me to use my creativity to the full."

If you would like to see how people like Kitch Davies can help you please call Laura Cahill on 0181 607 7700.

"Catering & Allied is leading the way with their people - no one else can match them."

CATERING & ALLIED

6. An opinion

7. Making the difference (i)

8. Making the difference (ii)

9. West Dean College dining room

Reproduced by kind permission of West Dean College

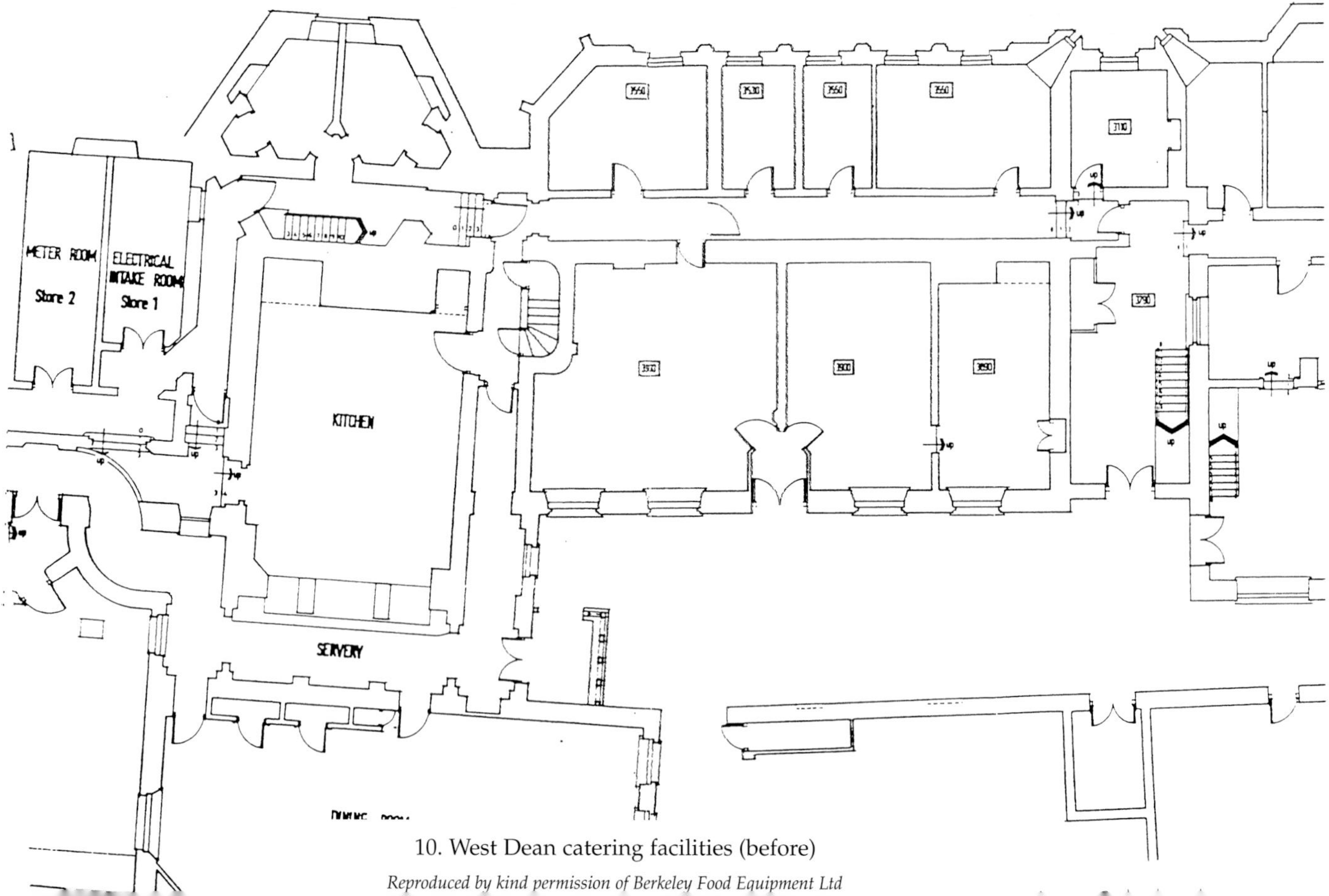

METER ROOM
Store 2
ELECTRICAL
INTAKE ROOM
Store 1
KITCHEN
SERVERY
3550
3530
3560
3560
3110
3570
3900
3890
3790
up

10. West Dean catering facilities (before)

Reproduced by kind permission of Berkeley Food Equipment Ltd

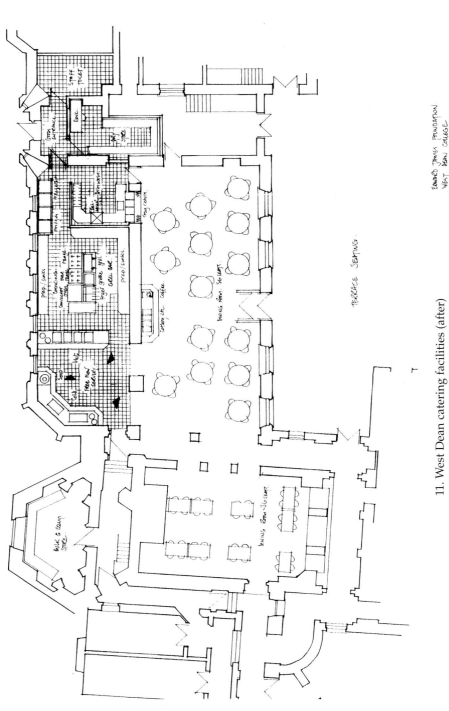

11. West Dean catering facilities (after)

Reproduced by kind permission of Berkeley Food Equipment Ltd

12. Strategic alliance

Reproduced by kind permission of PricewaterhouseCoopers

13. Strategic alliance

Reproduced by kind permission of Ferro Design

New Armouries Restaurant
New Armouries Building, Tower of London

General manager: Kevin Maher
Covers: 220 seats
Average spend: £4.20
Average daily covers: 1,200
Projected revenue: Year one £2.5m

PHOTOGRAPHS BY TOM STOCKILL

14. Digby Trout

Quality Catering Partners

Make the Difference

15. The QCP

Student of the Year
Competition & Conference

LAUSANNE

31 March - 4 April 1998

Lausanne

16. ECA Student of the Year literature

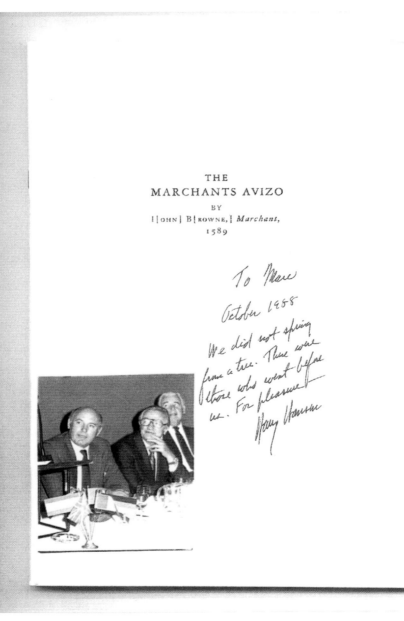

17. A personal dedication: Harry Hansen

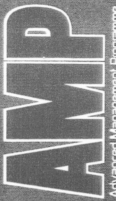

Advanced Management Programme

Professor Harry Hansen

DR. HARRY L. HANSEN

Malcolm P. McNair Professor of Marketing.

Harvard Graduate School of Business Administration.

Home: 1010 Memorial Drive, Cambridge, Massachusetts, 02138.

Education: Haverford College, S.B., 1933; Harvard Graduate School of Business Administration, M.B.A. with Distinction, 1935; Doctor of Commercial Science, 1939, De La Salle College (Philippines) Dr. Ed. in B.A. (Hon.) 1967.

Business and/or Teaching Experience: Harvard Graduate School of Business Administration: Research Assistant, 1935-36; Instructor, 1936-39; Assistant Dean, 1939-42; Assistant Professor, 1939-45; Associate Professor, 1945-49; Professor, 1949-; Director, Division of International Activities, 1963-65; Malcolm P. McNair Professor of Marketing, 1965 ; Harvard Business School Programme Advisor to Indian Institute of Management, Ahmedabad, India, 1963-68; Member Advisory Board Instituto de Estudios Superiores De La Empresa, Barcelona, Spain, 1963-; conducting management training programme in Ceylon, India, Hong Kong, Japan, Pakistan, Philippines, United Kingdom, Viet Nam, West Germany, 1956-.

Activities: Special consultant, Commanding General, United States Army Air Force, 1942-45. Member original faculty United States Army Air Force's Statistical Officers Candidate School 1942-45, Co-Director United States Army Air Force's War Adjustment (contract termination and surplus property diposal) Officers Course at Harvard, 1944-45. Scientific consultant, Office Field Services, Office of Scientific Research and Development, 1945. Member, Board of Alumni Advisors, Haverford College, 1953-55. Sports Illustrated's Silver All-American Award, 1957. Awarded Presidential Order of Merit, Republic of Philippines, 1973. Business and Foundation consultant. Corporate director.

Publications: "Problems in Marketing" (with M. P. McNair), McGraw-Hill Book Company, New York, 1949; "Readings in Marketing" (with M. P. McNair), McGraw-Hill Book Company, New York, 1949. Revised edition 1956. "Marketing Text, Cases and Readings," Richard D. Irwin, Inc., Chicago 1956. Rev. Ed. 1961; third edition 1987, fourth edition 1976 ; "British Managers in the Mirror" 1976.

Field: Business Policy, International Business. Marketing Management Development.

18. AMP: Harry Hansen

19. A Café Plus design

Our people –

The Telegraphists

Three long-serving members of our team at *The Telegraph* have enjoyed success with Catering & Allied, progressing along their respective career paths. **Lizzie Iworari-Sanya** initially worked as a temporary general assistant on the boat which served as the staff restaurant before the client moved to Canary Wharf Tower in 1992. Lizzie joined the permanent staff in 1987 and her interest in food and cooking was

Left to right: Lizzie Iworari-Sanya, Sarah Banner, Sylvia Donovan and Richard Lewis.

quickly recognised. She was encouraged to develop her skills by being promoted to assistant chef and enroling in college to study for City & Guilds 706/1 — to which she later added 706/2. She was promoted to chef de partie and later to night chef manager and then in 1994, Lizzie became sous chef in the Brasserie where she continues to develop her skills and her aim of eventually becoming head chef.

In 1989, **Richard Lewis** saw his role as a kitchen porter as a stopgap while he looked for a job as an art teacher. But his enthusiasm for food and cooking quickly grew and he asked if he could attend college to study for the NVQ levels 1 & 2 course. At the same time an opening occurred in the Brasserie kitchen for a trainee chef, which Richard was appointed to while the company sponsored his further education at college.

He has proved himself a dedicated team member and has recently taken on the roles of night and weekend chef. His art interest continues, giving him opportunities to design menus and backdrops for special days.

And when **Sylvia Donovan** joined as a general assistant in 1987, we were still running the catering service from a Portakabin. Earlier this year, Sylvia took on the new role as front of house supervisor in the Brasserie and, despite telling an interviewer on *The Telegraph*'s in-house magazine that her most frightening experience was 'being promoted', she has proved herself an extremely capable and worthy asset.

Computers and cabbages

Mike Wright, who has been with the company for nine years, is catering manager at Inmarsat, having started as a chef on the relief team and worked at several sites since. Currently Mike is working on a major computer project for Catering & Allied, trialling two stock control systems in four locations. The ultimate aim will be to introduce the preferred system throughout the business. In whatever spare time he can find, Mike is studying sales and marketing on a Hotel & Catering International Management Association (HCIMA) Distance Learning programme.

Laura Cahill was just 16 when she

Left to right: Ade Kole, Stuart Budgen, Laura Cahill and Mike Wright.

the secret ingredient

went to work as a general assistant at BICC, Mayfair. Now, ten years later, she is catering manager at Ford Warley. In between Laura has managed the deli bars at BICC and Dalgetty, been assistant manager at IBM and moved to Ford Warley as an assistant manager. While at BICC she joined the trainee manager programme and, with Catering & Allied help, began a part-time course to study for 706/1 and 2, a qualification which, she says, she has since found invaluable. Laura is now working with Sarah Banner visiting schools to tell children about the opportunities in the catering industry.

From kitchen porter to chef manager. That's the career history to date with Catering & Allied for **Ade Kole**, currently located at British Gas Tottenham Court Road. When he joined us at Heals in 1988 as a porter, helping the chef with veg prep, he thought he would like to become a chef himself. He was encouraged to develop his interest in food and enroled at Westminster College on day release to study NVQ 1 & 2. He moved later to British Gas, switching between the Marble Arch and Tottenham Court Road locations before being made chef manager. Ade is still studying at Westminster but has now moved up to the HCIMA final management course.

When **Stuart Budgen** started working as a kitchen porter at European Bank three years ago, he hadn't really decided what to do with his life and was looking for opportunities. He quickly found an interest in the work and Sandy Anderson tried to persuade him to train as a chef. But Stuart saw himself working front of house and when manager Rachel Lindner put him in charge of the espresso bar, he was soon looking for a chance to prove himself even more. Stuart is now a supervisor in the Mozart Restaurant and two evenings a week, with the help of Catering & Allied, he is studying on an HCIMA course at college, putting into practice during the day the management skills he is learning about in the classroom.

The Gastrophiles

Several of Catering & Allied's young chefs have benefitted from the teaching of **Sandy Anderson**, chef at the European Bank since it opened three-and-a-half years ago. Sandy helped get the current relief team

Back row l-r: Sandy Anderson, Tony Good, John Harris. Front l-r: Carlos Mistery and Rachel Lindner.

started and he will now have even more opportunity to help youngsters on their way as he joins with John Harris as a development chef. As well as working on new ideas for the company, he will continue to develop young chefs coming into the business.

But Sandy is also one of the leading lights behind Gastrophile, the company's food and wine 'club'. Designed for everybody in Catering & Allied to participate in, regardless of position or job,

Gastrophile is what Sandy describ as "a little bit of fun", talking abo food and drink together, sampli and demonstrating and trying ne and relevant menu ideas. Sandy loo after the demonstrations, aided a abetted by John Harris; Tony Go and Carlos Mistery are the drin experts; while Carlos also wor with Rachel Lindner to produce t Gastrophile news-letter. And ne year, Sandy says, they will be vent ing out of London on the Gastroph Road Show.

Head office too

It's not just out in the units that w have team members who have be with us for a number of years. O support staff at head office a around the areas are also playing major part in developing the bu ness. When **Siobhan Hunter** ca to Catering & Allied in 1987 as chef/manager on the relief team, s had already attained her HCIMA qu ifications and had experience other parts of the industry. Siobhan managed units and worked as an ope tions manager and has also achieved s tus as an Hotel & Catering Traini Company (HCTC) trainer to skill lev 2 and 3. Earlier this year, she came area work and was appointed as dev opment manager, with responsibility purchasing and product service dev opment. "After seven years of ope tions, it's great to have the opportun to do something new and it is ve exciting," Siobhan says.

Amanda White also joined the co pany in 1987, as a receptionist.

After about two years she was ask to support one of the regio field team as a secretary. Amar says she was given many oppo nities to develop her skills, cov ing for others while they were holiday and over the years she worked with most of the ope tional teams. Now, as well as lo ing after Digby Trout Restaura and administering for Cla Everson and Barry Moore, Amar is compiling information for sales database. She has had in nal training in computers and now in the process of collating much information as she can ga er.

Amanda White (left) and Siobhan Hunter.

(*What's Cooking*, Autumn 19

more experienced trainee chef managers fulfilling the role of assistant manager in two different units over a period of 18 months before taking charge of their own small units (i.e. feeding up to 50 people), running the kitchen and bookkeeping. In larger units, the chef and management functions were kept separate and it is interesting to note that, though it was possible for a chef to move into a solely administrative management role, it was likely in those days to be an unhappy transition because, as Banner notes, 'as a chef, you see things finished every day … you have a daily purpose, whereas as a manager you have an ongoing function'. All training was conducted under the auspices of the Hotel and Catering Training Board (HCTB), and Banner recalls how Sutcliffe's benefited from the grants awarded by that body through 'doing it their way' but also the disadvantages that inhered in the increasingly 'hidebound, red-taped' procedures. Over time, it became a 'very technical' process, and she found herself having to write 'complicated' programmes rather than being out in field alongside trainees.

In contrast, the Catering & Allied approach was marked by flexibility, a philosophy of working and developing *with*, together with, for example, sponsored day release for catering assistants wishing to study for City & Guilds qualifications such as 706/1&2 (cheffing). The training of managers, who already had either cheffing or catering qualifications, was similarly flexible, achieved via rotation through different kitchens and working alongside different chefs. This approach to training, very much driven by individual needs and aims, satisfied the HCTB whose advisor – having spoken with three or four unit managers about 'how they learned, were they happy, were they confident', and hearing that Sarah Banner and/or Vi Haire were always on hand to offer additional help if needed – approved the scheme, saying that, as Catering & Allied was a much smaller organization, there was no need for manuals or 'big, luxurious courses'. This approval was significant, for it ensured the granting of levy exemption from the HCTB, something that Verstringhe had sought from the outset.

From the beginning, the opportunities to develop and progress were available to personnel throughout the company. Part of the responsibility of unit managers was to identify and progress the potential of individuals, with all such initiatives supported by the modular management system in tandem with relevant training and education programmes. Thus, as shown in Box 5.1 below, with the necessary commitment and capability it was possible and practical for canteen assistants and kitchen porters to grow through the company into a variety of professional and managerial roles.

It is instructive to note the importance attached by Catering & Allied to celebrating achievement, from individual through to team and company. Incentives included the financial reward of sales leads but perhaps even more significant was the public expression of appreciation as conveyed for example by the company newsletter *What's Cooking*. Creativity and commitment were consistently profiled, with the above piece being just one example of effort recognized and encouraged within the context of company as both community and career enabler.

Laura Cahill recalls how she was asked at her original interview for the position of general assistant, aged just 16, how she saw her career developing within Catering & Allied. She said that she wanted to be a manager and, since 1996 when the above piece was written, has continued to build on every opportunity to fulfil this early ambition. After gaining further experience in business development within Hounslow head office, she was promoted in 1999 to group manager of the whole of the Catering & Allied Ford business, a contract which currently encompasses seven sites and two satellite groups, yields an annual turnover in excess of £3 million and employs a team of over 100. In noting her approach of working *with* the team and her perception of training and development of team members as key, the evolution of managers like Cahill may be seen in many ways to mirror that of Catering & Allied itself: realizing opportunities for progress that were yet predicated on the principle of total commitment, to client and company personnel alike.

From this perspective of investment in people, the steady growth of Catering & Allied created the impetus for a management training scheme for college graduates, with six being recruited to the programme each year. This involved three-month placements in four different units with the trainee acting as assistant manager, the unit manager working through the programme with them. A certificate was awarded on completion of the one year training period; all Catering & Allied training was in-house and never outside accredited. This scheme, initiated in 1988, combined the benefits of several approaches to personal development: demonstration, coaching, mentoring, and rotation through a different roles. It was clearly oriented towards creating the competencies staff required to work effectively within a flexible team mode of operation, in a customized environment.

The success of the company approach to training and quality assurance was ultimately and formally recognized with the Investors in People (IiP) accreditation, first awarded in August 1996. The assessment report includes, *inter alia*, a list of training and development activities salient amongst which are:

- Coaching skills for unit managers
- Formal team building training for unit managers
- 'Assured safe catering' for unit managers, head chefs, and assistant managers cascaded to all staff
- 'Advanced food hygiene' training for unit managers cascaded to all staff
- 'Colour me beautiful' image consultancy for unit managers cascaded to unit staff
- In-house customer care training for all staff
- 'Health & hygiene' certificated two day course for all staff
- 'Basic food handling' course for all staff
- 'Food monitoring' training for all staff
- 'Healthy eating' awareness raising for all staff

It is clear that every member of staff was given the opportunity to acquire a comprehensive knowledge base that could be built on and developed according to particular competences and interests. This learning element is clearly articulated in the IiP 'Conclusion and Recommendation':

Catering & Allied have always been a learning organisation – it was one of their founding core values, and Investors in

People has given them a structure for their processes. The managing director stated that Catering & Allied is first and foremost a 'people business' and that the 'process was more important than the badge'. ... When asked 'who are your key people', the chairman replied ... 'the people closest to the client', i.e. the unit staff. ... Catering & Allied certainly have the right culture, philosophy, and approach, and some very strong and embedded systems. They commit the resources, plan well, and undertake lots of activities and test the effectiveness on a number of levels. They are doing enough to be judged as an Investor in People.

Open communications and relationship building were clearly key in the learning process, both within the organization and across the customer/service provider boundary. The team philosophy clearly emanated from the company executive; Marc Verstringhe, Kit Cuthbert and Vi Haire worked together in selling the business from start up, whilst Sarah Banner and Vi Haire formed a key partnership through first, in the earlier days, opening and running new units until managers could be recruited, and later in facilitating, monitoring and supporting the work of the in-house teams. From the perspective of customer relations, Verstringhe, Cuthbert, Haire and Banner would visit units on a regular basis, encouraging managers to talk to the customers, and clients to facilitate communication between their staff and the caterers. In depth surveys of customer opinion would generally take place in a unit once a year, involving managers from other units and thereby effecting a cross-fertilization of ideas between facilities, whilst any problems would be addressed as soon as they presented. Banner notes that, for various reasons, an 'invisible barrier' could sometimes emerge between the customers and catering staff, and communications were vital in resolving this issue. In one such case, involving a large client with multiple units, she headed up a team that spent three days talking to customers about their preferences and concerns and subsequently holding feedback meetings with the unit managers so that the situation – in this case, involving the nature of the food, which it transpired was deemed 'too fancy' - could be adjusted. The problem was resolved, and the contract has been retained to the present day.

This example clearly illustrates the modular management system in operation; elements of monitoring and control are evident, but within a wider context of participation. Heller et al (1998: 65) point up the essence of organization as

> The enhancement of individual effort through the differentiated and integrated work of many and at the same time the constraint of coordinated cooperation imposed upon individual will and representation.

As discussed in Chapter Four, the individualism of in-house unit managers was actively encouraged by the patron driven philosophy of Catering & Allied, with support and 'enhancement of effort' deriving from an essentially participative approach to management, enabled by a flexible, modular framework. A key element in this framework, complementing that of quality and assurance and training, was that of operations management.

The modular management system: Operations management

A significant figure in establishing and directing the Catering & Allied operations system was Vi Haire. Following an early career with the Grosvenor House in Park Lane, during which time she gained a City & Guilds diploma in hotel management and hands-on experience of a range of duties including advance bookings, stocktaking, bar work and housekeeping (NB in those days, i.e. the late 1950s, women were not permitted to go 'front of house' in West End hotels), Haire then ran a country hotel and subsequently a public house in Knightsbridge, before joining the Law Society as assistant manager for all catering functions in 1967. During the banqueting season in particular, the workload was heavy - 10.00 a.m-2.00 a.m., six days per week – and, after three years, Haire took the decision to move into industrial catering, where the hours were much shorter. She was recruited to Sutcliffe London by Marc Verstringhe in 1970, as co-manager of the in-house facility of a television company. She found it difficult, in the early days; the environment was very different to her previous experience and her prior knowledge of industrial catering was based on anecdote: 'When people said they could produce a meal for 1/6 (8p), we nearly fainted. It really was the poor end of the industry'.

Within her first unit, Haire was jointly responsible for a morning coffee round to the offices, followed by lunch for between 300/400, afternoon tea and a supper service. Getting good quality catering assistants was 'very, very difficult' – on one occasion, the lady who assisted with the morning coffee put salt out instead of sugar! Altogether, with her co-manager, Haire was responsible for between 30 and 40 catering staff, in a large and complex operation.

After ten months, in 1971, she was promoted to area supervisor, in charge of ten units, and subsequently to area manager, with responsibility for 'around 40/50 units – far too many', with three area supervisors reporting in to her. Her own direct report was to Kit Cuthbert, the one who first approached Haire with the idea of joining the proposed new company with a somewhat oblique question that, for the latter, came 'out of the blue': 'Are you afraid of responsibility?' Haire at that stage was unaware of the plans under discussion but, when she was offered the post of operations manager in the autumn of 1975, decided to accept. Up until that point, she had thought that five years is 'long enough' in any organization, and had been thinking about a change, having been with Sutcliffe's for that period; she was, however, to remain with Catering & Allied for the rest of her working life, progressing from operations manager to operations director in a career with the company that spanned over 20 years.

When starting up the company, the aim was to eliminate a whole layer of management from the Sutcliffe model. Thus, there was a reduction in the number of units that an area manager looked after (which could be as many as 50 within Sutcliffe's); Haire considered 20 to be the maximum viable number and this became the norm, with each block of units managed by an operations manager with the support of a field operator who had responsibility for the day to day work, rotating through each of the units on a four weekly basis. The relationship between operations manager and field operator was key; as Haire notes, the work necessitated a partnership, and it was also a fundamental responsibility of the former to grow, and develop, the latter, who would be looking to progress into a management role. Thus, the field operator would be involved in all aspects of the management function; for example, at the monthly budget meetings with the client, the field operator would prepare the figures and formally present them to the client together with the operations manager or operations director. Haire's philosophy is clear: 'You can't grow people unless you involve them. A lot of people keep knowledge to themselves. But I believe, if you're in a team, that the team should know exactly what's going on, from top to bottom. Everybody should understand where you are. You shouldn't have an ops manager who does not tell a field operator what their thinking is'.

Apart from budgeting and monitoring client accounts, the operations manager's areas of responsibility included client and customer relationships, approving and selecting key staff (particularly in-house managers), and innovations from an overall perspective. Haire notes that an operations manager 'should take an overview', looking at the whole picture and identifying those parts within it where service could be improved.

> You need to look at something as a whole; if you've got an area, you should be able to plan it. You should have progression. The ops manager should have progression planning *within their area* (NB an important point, otherwise it impinges on the job of the operations director). But the ops managers are there to look at their area and build in progression, so you have the big units in which you have several managers and assistant managers who can then be moved into the next slot. So if you look at it like pigeonholes, you should be moving it about – and there's never enough time for that sort of thing; people don't give enough time to thought.

This issue of time is critical; Haire's perception of the contract catering industry overall was that there was not enough thought given to what people actually did, mainly because of time constraints. These increase with growth; in the case of Catering & Allied, for example, Sarah Banner notes that whilst, in the early days, there was time to work alongside unit teams, perhaps following up a concern of Vi Haire's, or maybe just through 'dropping in', as the company grew she had to adopt a 'tick box' system for quality assurance which, though she disliked it, was efficient and far less time intensive.

The development of Haire's role illustrates the possibilities for reconciling two positive management policies, which of themselves are contradictory. On the one hand it is desirable, especially in a company providing personal service, for managers to remain close to the customer and front-line staff by keeping their spans of control low. On the other hand, limiting spans of control will increase the layers of management, unless compensating action is taken. It is desirable, for well-known reasons, to keep the number of management layers to a minimum. The way that Catering & Allied reconciled these two desirables was to move responsibility as far down as possible, and to rely as much as was thought possible on self-management. By decentralizing management tasks, and outsourcing many functions supporting the main service-providing activities, Catering & Allied found a solution to this common dilemma. This initiative formed part of the company's 'partnership' concept, which attempted to translate a vertical relationship into that of a team, as we shall see shortly.

Decentralization was essential for Haire to 'take an overview'. Only by freeing herself up from other responsibilities could Vi and others in Catering & Allied's management adopt a sufficiently broad perspective as to make sure that activities of longer-term significance to the company were not forced away from their attention by an over-involvement in operational decisions. Client relations, including careful attention to feedback from the customer, and service innovation are significant examples of such attention to longer-term issues. Yet at the same time, the way forward had to be informed by a first-hand knowledge of what people actually do, and here the early decision to limit area managers' spans of control was essential.

There is one particularly interesting example that illustrates the point concerning 'what people actually do' and the need to take time to consider this. In the first experiment with link manning, another element of the unique organizational structure and process of Catering & Allied that is discussed in detail below, Sarah Banner notes that the four girls who rotated through cooking and food preparation were a deliberate mix of City and

Guilds with Cordon Bleu, 'because the latter understood food, had a lot of bubble and came from a different background, much chattier, whereas the former had the skills, and the speed, and the finish. The whole lot would blend together'. Furthermore, beyond this 'blending', the arrangement also created a valuable opportunity for skills and knowledge transfer over time.

Link manning: An experiment in work organization

In Chapter Four, we considered the philosophy of Catering & Allied concerning customer relations and the strategies developed by the company to fulfil its stated 'total commitment to client satisfaction'. This section focuses on the interaction of structure and process in service delivery, applying theories of work organization in the analysis of a key element within the organization: the in-house catering team led by the unit manager.

In his classic exposition of the 'human organization', Likert (1967) identifies four discrete management systems of which system 4 is the most productive. This particular system depends on, *inter alia*:

- complete confidence and trust in all matters subsisting between team members and management

- free communication flow – down, up, and with peers

- full involvement of team members in all decisions related to their work

- constructive use of all team members' opinions and ideas, with personnel at all levels feeling responsibility for organization's goals

- all social forces – both formal and informal – supporting efforts to achieve the shared goals

The principle of supportive relationships is fundamental to this system of management, originally formulated by Likert in 1961:

The leadership and other processes of the organization must be such as to ensure a maximum probability that in all interactions and in all relationships within the organization, each member, in the light of his background, values, desires, and expectations, will view the experience as supportive and one which builds and maintains his sense of personal worth and importance

(1961: 103)

Taking Likert's System 4 as the point of departure for their empirical research into goal setting, Latham and Saari (1979) demonstrate the significance of supportive relationships in the process and the correlation between participatively set goals and 'better' performance when compared with that resulting from assigned or 'do your best' goals. The authors conclude that 'participation appears to be important in that it increases understanding of task requirements (p 151). Again, as noted by Mohrman et al (1995: 20), 'social outcomes are optimised when the team has responsibility for a "whole" task and enjoys autonomy, variety, and meaningfulness of work'.

This team approach to work organization is central to recent thinking on 'high-performance work systems'. It involves extensive participation by the members of work groups or teams in how their work is arranged. Team members are provided with adequate information for them to manage themselves, including the interfaces with higher management and the other parties the team relates to in its activities. Depending on where the team is located in the value chain, these other parties might include clients and suppliers, as well as other teams that are 'upstream' and 'downstream' in the flow of work. The principles behind high performance work systems are those of maximum autonomy and minimum formal design, so allowing teams and work groups to learn, evolve and adjust to changing needs largely through their own volition. Wellins and his colleagues (1994) provide detailed examples of how these principles have been applied to teams.

Teamwork brings a number of advantages. By substituting a peer-based control of work for hierarchical control, it has been found to increase employees' sense of accountability and responsibility. One of the associated effects is a reduction in absenteeism as team members become more committed to what they are doing. Teamwork permits employees to pool their ideas so as to come up with better and more creative solutions to problems. The combination of mutual adjustment by the team and the encouragement for its members to be creative, in turn increases the speed of response to new requirements and the company's flexibility in general. A further benefit lies in the way that teamwork enables a company to remove hierarchical layers and cut its administrative overheads. This last advantage was clearly in line with one of Catering & Allied's basic tenets.

The conditions that experience has shown to be necessary to move successfully towards effective teamwork are also consistent with the Catering & Allied philosophy. One fundamental requirement is to avoid an association in employees' minds between high-performance work systems and loss of employment. Innovations in work organization and productivity improvement will not be sustained if workers fear this will lead them to work themselves out of a job. Management must also be prepared to trust its staff with genuinely greater autonomy and responsibility. This includes a willingness to grant staff real initiative and also to share the information necessary for them to use initiative responsibly. It is also necessary to support moves in this direction with the careful selection of people who are capable and happy to take on more responsibility and work flexibly, adequate training, and adjustments to payment systems so as to bring these in line with a team mode of organization and assessment (Parker and Wall, 1998; Pfeffer, 1998).

The concepts thus far identified in respect of team working towards shared goals, especially in respect of positive social outcomes and mutually supportive relationships, are particularly pertinent to a service industry such as catering in which the 'cross counter bond' (*Office Equipment Index*, March 1984) can only be created and sustained through an integrated team approach predicated on a common goal. In the case of Catering & Allied, the company philosophy of commitment to client and staff alike, with the concept of working *with* rather than *for*, is clearly enacted in the link-manning approach to customer service.

Link-manning was initiated in 1978 by the unit manager of CDP which, as noted in Chapter Four, was also the first Catering & Allied facility to offer a bistro/wine bar style of staff catering. Traditionally, catering operations have been run on a pyramid structure with manager and deputy, head chef, second chef and catering assistants. Duties and responsibilities are attached to each post and are carried out by the incumbent. Link manning abandons the rigidity of the traditional structure and substitutes a flexible approach using predominantly skilled staff in which each person is not just trained to carry out a variety of functions but actually rotates through jobs so that, over time, he or she develops expertise in most of the disciplines involved in running the operation. Communication between management, team members and customers flows more freely as no-one is locked into a particular task, further enabling the participative setting of goals; for example, the ongoing planning and development of menus through chef/customer interaction and feedback.

There are two main advantages to this approach to customer service. From the perspective of catering staff, interest and job satisfaction is sustained through the opportunities for learning and, ultimately, career progression it presents; the hands-on experience and acquisition of explicit knowledge is complemented by programmes of business and academic learning in the context of a supportive management structure. From the point of view of production and its budgetary implications, link manning is also extremely efficient. In a conventional catering operation, typically only three out of ten people are skilled, a ratio that is reversed in the link manning approach. The resultant 'skilling up' yields an improvement in productivity of around 30% such that, for similar staffing costs, food and service quality is greatly increased.

The following table represents the original link manning operation devised by the unit manager of CDP, demonstrating a full cycle of job rotation over three weeks. There were just four staff, serving a total of 120 lunches, in the ratio of 3:1 skilled/unskilled (A=unit manager/chef; B=chef; C=chef; and porter). The cooking was rostered as follows:

No 1:   Main meal vegetables and soup. Bread and garlic bread

No 2:   Four main cold courses

No 3:   Salads and sweets. Make up vinaigrette, mayonnaise, etc, for next day. Chop parsley

Running a restaurant facility does not only entail cheffing, however; the following schedules also incorporate a cleaning roster, represented throughout by the number 1, which was routinely fulfilled as follows:

Monday:	Oven
Tuesday:	Cupboards
Wednesday:	Refrigerators
Thursday:	Drawers and shelves for saucepans
Friday:	Restaurant tables and mirrors; extra cleaning of hot cupboard and bainmarie

Additional duties comprised the following:

No 1: Clean all work surfaces, window ledges, fronts of cupboards, fridges, stock cupboard. Tops and fronts of ovens. Tiled surfaces over oven and sinks. Main sink and wash hand basin. Coffee machine

Nos 2 & 3: Serve on counter, clear tables, clean shelves, bainmarie hot cupboard, etc. Help porter if busy

Duty Roster CDP (1978)

Week 1

	Monday	Tuesday	Wednesday	Thursday	Friday
A	1	3	2	1	3
B	2	1	3	2	1
C	3	2	1	3	2

Week 2

	Monday	Tuesday	Wednesday	Thursday	Friday
A	2	1	3	2	1
B	3	2	1	3	2
C	1	3	2	1	3

Week 3

	Monday	Tuesday	Wednesday	Thursday	Friday
A	3	2	1	3	2
B	1	3	2	1	3
C	2	1	3	2	1

In this way, each member of the team not only developed expertise in a wide range of culinary skills but shared fully in what may be seen perhaps as less appealing duties, such as cleaning the oven. There is no hierarchy in this example of work organization; the unit manager operated as a member of the team in an eminently flexible approach that was swiftly adopted throughout all other Catering & Allied facilities, moulded and tailored to larger operations also.

Pfeffer (1994: 6) notes the changing basis of competitive success, in that

> traditional sources of success – product and process technology, protected or regulated markets, access to financial resources, and economies of scale – can still provide competitive leverage, but to a lesser degree now than in the past, leaving *organizational culture and capabilities, derived from how people are managed, as comparatively more vital.* (Italics added)

In the team approach encapsulated by the link manning principle, with the flexibility to innovate in the development and realization of shared goals, we see the competitive advantage of a 'work force that has the ability to achieve competitive success and that cannot be readily duplicated by others' (Pfeffer 1994: 21). Paradoxically, the creation of such unique associations or 'work forces' can be seen in part to depend on the development of *individual* capabilities that are yet shaped, motivated and integrated by an overarching organizational philosophy. In a later work, Pfeffer identifies as one of seven practices of successful organization the 'self managed team and decentralization of decision making as ... basic principles of organizational design' (1998: 96). This observation raises issues of autonomy and control; the author goes on to note that 'teams substitute peer-based for hierarchical control of work ... Peer control is frequently more effective than hierarchical supervision' (ibid: 104/105). This points up the organizational variable identified by Likert in respect of the extent to which review and control functions are concentrated; in respect of the most productive management system, System 4, he finds:

Quite widespread responsibility for review and control, with lower units at times imposing more rigorous reviews and tighter controls than top management

(Likert, 1967: 9)

From the perspective of top management within Catering & Allied, such ground level control was critical within individual catering facilities. Following the company's accreditation by West London TEC as an Investor in People (August 1996), an interview with quality assurance and training director Sarah Banner noted that:

The catering policy and staff must be hand-in-glove with the host organization. The only way to do this effectively is to devolve authority down to the site manager and their staff. It would not be possible for the directors in headquarters to fine-tune each restaurant – that has to be left to the people on the spot.

This chapter has considered two elements of the unique organizational structure and process of Catering & Allied: the supportive and participative modular management system, enabling the effective devolution of authority to in-house managers and their teams, and the innovative link-manning approach to service delivery. The third is the extensive network of strategic alliances developed by the company over time. In essence, these three elements combined improved the margin by 7% and productivity by 35%; in the BHA 2000 survey, the last in which a direct comparison may be made between Catering & Allied and its competitors, Catering & Allied is shown to have achieved £34,391 sales per person employed (with senior management) compared with global leader Compass at £25,154 and Halliday Catering, a smaller operator, at £22,185.

Throughout its history, Catering & Allied maintained a lean core structure; for example, the company had no HRM department, no central buying function, no planning and design division, and no in-house secretariat. Instead, expertise was bought in as and when required, in a fluid, open and flexible system that was also highly cost effective. The philosophy and evolution of this approach is discussed in the following chapter.

References

Barney, J B (1991). 'Firm resources and sustained competitive advantage'. *Journal of Management*, 17: 99-120

British Hospitality Association *Contract Catering Survey* 2000

Caterer & Hotelkeeper, 24 May 2001

Doherty, L (2001). 'Contract catering – stunning, fantastic, the best!'. *The Hospitality Review*, January: 37-41

Hartley, B and M W Starkey (eds) (1996). *The management of sales and customer relations*. London: International Thomson Business Press

Heller, F, E Pusi_, G Strauss and B Wilpert (1998). *Organizational participation: Myth and reality*. Oxford: OUP

Latham, G P and L M Saari (1979). 'Importance of supportive relationships in goal setting'. *Journal of Applied Psychology*, 64/2: 151-156

Likert, R (1967). *The human organization: Its management and value*. New York: McGraw Hill

Likert, R (1961). *New patterns of management*. New York: McGraw Hill

McKenna, E F and N Beech (1995). *The essence of human resource management*. Hemel Hempstead: Prentice-Hall

Mahoney, J and J R Pandian (1992). 'The resource-based view within the conversation of strategic management'. *Strategic Management Journal*, 13: 363-380

Mohrman, S A, S G Cohen and A M Mohrman Jr (1995). *Designing team-based organizations: New forms for knowledge work*. San Francisco: Jossey-Bass

Nonaka, I and H Takeuchi (1995). *The knowledge creating company*. Oxford: OUP

Office Equipment Index (1984). 'Good presentation is the proof of the pudding', March

Parker, S and T Wall (1998). *Job and work design: Organizing work to promote well-being and effectiveness*. Thousand Oaks: Sage.

Pfeffer, J (1998). 'Seven practices of successful organizations'. *California Management Review*, 40/2: 96-124

Pfeffer, J (1994). *Competitive advantage through people: Unleashing the power of the work force*. Boston: Harvard Business School Press

Stone, R J (2002). *Human Resource Management*. Milton, Qld: Wiley Australia.

Wellins, R S, W C Byham and G R Dixon (1994). *Inside teams: How 20 world-class organizations are winning through teamwork*. San Francisco: Jossey-Bass.

What's Cooking, Spring 1996

What's Cooking, June 1988

Chapter Six

Managing Partnerships and Organizational Boundaries

The formation of partnerships and alliances has become an increasingly popular means for companies to realize their strategic objectives. As a result, the field of study known as cooperative strategy came into fashion during the 1990s, following the attention that had been accorded to competitive strategy during the 1980s (Faulkner and de Rond, 2000). Taking a broad perspective, partnerships between companies, and indeed between different units within a company, form part and parcel of the moves to overcome organizational boundaries that gave rise to the concept of the 'boundaryless corporation' (Devanna and Tichy, 1990). The dissolution of boundaries through partnership was regarded as a particularly promising way for companies to secure a competitive advantage by being faster than their competitors in satisfying customer needs and generally adapting to new environmental demands.

Partnerships can take a wide variety of forms. Within a company, considerable benefits can be derived from the creating an active partnership between different departments through the creation of teams. Such teams can provide a focus on meeting customer requirements that might well otherwise be lacking. People working within the bounds of their own departments or units naturally tend to give priority to the particular objectives and standards rather than to the wider goal of competing in the marketplace. Cross-functional teams are therefore often established in order to create a customer-oriented mindset and to enable the team members to reorganize their work so as to realize that orientation with economy and speed, as customers require (Wellins et al., 1994). It has also be found that the bringing together of different functional or specialist staff to work in teams with an agreed objective to accomplish, provides a powerful organizational tool for generating innovation and superior problem solutions. In other words, partnerships through teams can be a powerful aid to organizational learning (Edmondson, 1999). It is not surprising that Catering & Allied, a company that placed a premium on both customer service and learning, was one of the earliest to adopt in-house teams, as the previous chapter has described.

This chapter looks at the partnerships that Catering & Allied formed with other companies and outside professionals and specialists. Partnerships between organizations or units can range from informal collaborations not necessarily based on any contract, through various contractual arrangements governing specified joint activities, to investing equity in a newly created joint venture enterprise. Unfortunately, people do not apply a consistent terminology to these various possibilities, though they all fall under the umbrella of what is commonly called a strategic alliance. This simply denotes that fact that a company enters into partnership with others in the belief that it can thereby meet its strategic objectives better than by operating alone. If they are successful, partnerships often evolve from a lower level of commitment to a higher level. For example, companies that have achieved a period of successful collaboration on joint projects and information exchange may well decide to deepen their mutual commitment through a swap of equity.

Many partnerships between companies have a short life. Surveys suggest that between 40 and 50% are terminated within five years. These percentages are inflated by the fact that some terminations should not be judged as failures, when for instance the partners have achieved their joint objectives and part amicably or when one partner agrees to its share being bought out by the other (Child and Faulkner, 1998). Nevertheless, the high rate of termination indicates that partnerships can be difficult to sustain and depend on a number of important conditions for their potential to be realized. These conditions fall into two broad categories. One is whether there is a clear logic for the partnership so that each partner needs the other(s). This is sometimes known as the 'strategic fit' between the partners. The other concerns how well the partners learn to work together. Here mutual confidence and trust play a very large role.

Strategic fit

The fundamental issue with strategic fit is whether the partnership can better achieve strategic gains for the partners than would be available if they did not collaborate. Partnerships can offer a number of strategic gains depending on circumstances, and these potential gains provide the motives behind them (Contractor and Lorange, 1988):

1. to reduce risks, such as those attaching to investment in innovation;

2. to exchange technology or other mutually useful knowledge;

3. to achieve economies of scale and/or rationalization;

4. to enable a company to focus on its core competencies and to remain correspondingly smaller than otherwise;

5. to link companies with complementary competencies or assets in a value chain;

6. to co-opt or block competition;

7. to facilitate the international expansion of inexperienced firms;

8. to overcome government-mandated trade or investment barriers.

The strategic fit between prospective partners is therefore a question of how well they could bring together complementary assets in ways that would enhance their mutual competitive advantage. Even the last mentioned benefit, to overcome governmental trade or investment barriers in effect places a domestic partner in the position of offering a strategic asset to a foreign partner seeking to enter its market. In many cases, the full benefit of partners' complementary assets can only be realized if the ways they work together creates a true synergy between them. This places a premium on how well the partnership is managed, so that each party is willing to share its knowledge and skills and its staff are prepared to work together openly and constructively. In this way, what is sometimes called the cultural fit of a partnership becomes a necessary condition for its strategic potential to be fully realized.

Cultural fit: identity and trust

One would expect that a carefully planned partnership will be founded on sound logic, with the potential to show considerable strategic gains. The partners should therefore be highly motivated to make a success of it. Yet it may underachieve, and even founder, if friction develops between the partners. It is quite normal for some difference of views to arise because part of the logic of partnership lies in differences between the parties. Without differences there would be no grounds for complementarity and little potential for mutual learning. Partners will therefore come together with different organizational and sometimes national cultures, which translate into contrasting norms of communicating, organizing and working.

The ability to achieve an acceptable fit between such contrasting cultures is a vital requirement for the management of successful partnerships. A lot of the responsibility for achieving this fit, and the synergy it can encourage, rests with the senior managers of the partner companies, and with the general manager of a joint venture if one is created. The issue comes down to one of managing the relations between the key personnel involved and generating a sense of common purpose among them. Two requirements for generating this sense of common purpose are to forge a shared identity between the partners, and to build on this so as to foster trust between them.

One of the paradoxes underlying partnerships is that they can be preferred over full-scale mergers or acquisitions because they preserve the separate identities of the partners. The submersion of these identities to a degree sufficient to creation an identity for a partnership sufficient to grant it salience, and particularly to realize potential synergies, will therefore need to be handled with sensitivity (Child and Rodrigues, 2003). If the partners are collaborating in just a limited way, perhaps confined to exchanging information or achieving cost savings by pooling resources, the achievement of synergy may not be on the agenda. In this situation, separate identities can readily be preserved and the issue may not be a sensitive one. It is likely to become more sensitive when the partners seek to evolve their collaboration further in ways that require some sublimation of their separate identities. This will arise if they establish joint organizational arrangements, undertake joint innovation, or pursue a common strategy. The creation of a sense of joint identity at this deeper level of collaboration will provide a firm basis for mutual trust.

Trust is the ultimate requirement for a successfully running partnership (Child, 2001). Managers are discovering the key role that mutual trust plays in the success of partnership and joint projects. Formal contracts play a necessary part in establishing the conditions and performance milestones for collaboration, and they may provide the only basis on which business partners are prepared to work together in the first instance. But such contracts are rarely enough by themselves. Informal understanding, based on trust, often proves to be a more powerful factor in determining how the collaboration works out. Of course, trust is itself likely to be reinforced by a successful relationship and this virtuous circle is an ideal one, if it can be obtained.

It is not therefore surprising that people engaged in all areas of business and industry, and in every country, say they value trust and trustworthiness as a basis for partnership. At the same time, they recognize that it is not an easy thing to obtain. As a senior executive of a leading IT systems services company involved in a range of strategic alliances commented:

No partnership will work without trust and it is one of the most difficult things to achieve.

A second example shows, nevertheless, that trust can be built up and can place a partnership on a very solid foundation. It concerns a UK industrial printing company, one of the technologically most advanced in the world, which undertook a joint development project with its US subsidiary, a large American customer and a specialist printing materials supplier. The project aimed to develop the effective application of rapid industrial printing using the laser technology possessed by its US subsidiary. It was therefore a central plank in the company's strategy. The partnership it created was based entirely on trust and goodwill – no contract was signed. The UK company's technical director commented:

We were able to achieve the benefits of collaboration as a consequence of the personal relationships that built up, that recognized we could be more exploratory, that we could understand each other's good and bad points...This is an informal relationship which has simply developed out of a mutual wish to move the business forward and from an adequate level of trust in each other's goodwill.

Partnerships clearly present managers with new requirements because of the way they aim to bring together people who are not previously familiar with working together, have different identities, and may perceive that their interests do not coincide. Given that there is sound logic behind a partnership in the first place and that the partners are therefore motivated to work together, its success depends fundamentally on the quality of personal relations between those involved. This means that careful attention must be given to issues of identity and trust. It is a formidable managerial challenge and many mistakes are made.

Catering & Allied accumulated a valuable experience of partnerships at three levels. As discussed in Chapter Five, partnerships within the company have taken the form of teams. At a second level, the company developed business teams based on what it calls 'strategic alliances' between its staff and external partners including designers, suppliers, and especially the client. The third level of partnership has been mainly with other European catering companies. Catering & Allied began as an Anglo-Dutch alliance; this later extended to a wider European alliance with four partners. This chapter now describes the rationales behind the strategic alliances and European catering partnership, as well as how they were managed.

The Catering & Allied strategic alliance concept

The strategic alliance concept evolved from an approach first adopted in 1966 at Sutcliffe Catering. Having been successful in winning the contract for Honeywell Controls in Brentford, there was a need to re-design and equip the kitchen in order to provide for the combo system of catering. Sutcliffe had chosen to replace the service Honeywell had previously received from the Four Square Company whose system was based on frozen and convenience foods. The essence of the combo system is to provide a cuisine based on fresh foods combined with some convenience foods. This required the kitchen to be larger than one used for frozen foods. A problem arose because there was not enough space available.

To brainstorm the challenge, Verstringhe and his colleagues

sought the expertise of an outside specialist designer. His name was Chris Nutt, with whom Sutcliffe had carried out a number of successful projects before. Chris had impressed with his innovative way of thinking, his style of drawing and his skills as an engineer. More importantly, Chris was able to work together with the Sutcliffe people as a team despite the fact that he was a service supplier. He shared the same enthusiasm and commitment to the task. The outcome was the first combo system location at Honeywell Controls, which is described in the next chapter. The development of the combo system was the basis for a subsequent rapid expansion of business for the Sutcliffe Catering London Company.

When Catering & Allied was founded in 1975, it seemed logical to continue with this approach of working with outside specialists. Later on, it became known in business as 'outsourcing'. Outsourcing spread widely as a business practice during the 1990s. It was inspired by the advice to focus on core competencies (Hamel and Prahalad 1994), though in practice it was often driven by the desire to cut costs and achieve downsizing. The thinking at Catering & Allied foreshadowed the idea of core competencies in that it recognized how the company's ability to offer a superior service to the client could be strengthened by bringing in skills from outside to complement its own resources. This approach proved particularly effective as the main objective at Catering & Allied was to bring some excitement to eating at the workplace by creating restaurants rather than clinical cafeterias or canteens. This meant introducing colour, style and a congenial atmosphere.

This concept, which the company called the 'strategic alliance', grew as its business expanded. With a view to meeting the requirements of its different clients, the strategic alliance approach provided an opportunity to bring in different styles, furniture and atmosphere to each new project. Catering & Allied therefore did not just work with one specialist designer but with a number in order to achieve the variety and diversity it sought. It worked with specialists like Fergus Stapleton of Ferro Design and Ron Hodge of Servequip, the latter of whom was originally in hygiene and began in business importing Italian catering equipment into the UK. He first met Verstringhe in 1965 and 'sold the Italian concept' to him, supplying all the Sutcliffe outlets and gradually expanding into planning, design and ultimately turnkey projects, involving total fit out.

An example of the strategic alliance approach of Catering & Allied is provided by the design and planning of the new Abacus staff restaurant facility for Coopers and Lybrand in 1986 (see Box 6.1).

6.1 The strategic alliance: partnership for an innovative solution

Coopers and Lybrand was in the mid-1980s a long established city accountancy and management consultancy practice. In October 1985, it had moved into its new headquarters in Plumtree Court, London. The building contained seven client-entertaining suites with a full kitchen, but there was no available space for a fully equipped staff restaurant. Initially, the staff were offered a temporary canteen facility with low-cost snacks supplemented by a sandwich-vending service sited throughout the building. It was the firm's ambition, however, to provide its staff with a proper restaurant, recognizing that relatively few facilities were available outside and that it would also provide an important social meeting point for people to meet who were often away from the office for considerable periods of time.

When a basement 60-seater lunch or dining room and nightclub became available next door in Spring 1986, it provided an opportunity to create a restaurant facility. From the outset, it was decided that the restaurant should be of high quality in which design, food and service would all be of the highest standard. Unlike most staff restaurants, it was decided that it should have a name – Abacus. Catering & Allied were already on site catering in the client-entertaining suites, but they had to tender for the new brief in competition with other companies. The basis of the brief was that the contractor appointed should provide a turnkey package in which they would be responsible for four main items:

1. the design and fitting of the kitchen and restaurant;
2. the installation of specialist equipment;

---

3. the delivery of food programmes to a predetermined budget;

4. the eventual management and staffing of the restaurant.

Catering & Allied won the contract. According to Cooper and Lybrand's director of administration, this was on the basis of its overall management structure, the quality of its staff, its innovative design approach, its economic operating costs and its link-manning procedure.

The design for the 3500 square foot Abacus restaurant was jointly developed through a strategic alliance between Catering & Allied, the Ferro Design Group, and the specialist Servequip company providing design input for the kitchen: the selection of food preparation units, ovens and food-holding equipment. Throughout the two-month period of building and refurbishment, there were regular weekly meetings involving the client, contractor and subcontractors to review progress and to take decision on such matters as fabrics, fittings, wallpapers, crockery and cutlery. The close working relationship resulting from these meetings, together with other discussions where necessary, led to two positive results. First, time was never wasted waiting for the client's decision; this could be conveyed on the spot. Second, all parties were fully informed about the various aspects of the project.

The outcome of this 'strategic alliance' between Catering & Allied, contractors and the client was a high quality staff restaurant with genuine character. The innovative use of devices such as sliding panels, movable serving counters and variable lighting enabled its atmosphere and functions to change at different times of the day.

Application of Catering & Allied's link-manning rota ensured that the restaurant's staff had responsibility for more than one set of agreed tasks. This flexibility enabled them to vary their work schedule, covered for unforeseen contingencies, and retain a high level of interest through being involved with different aspects of the catering function.

Source: Nigel Anker, 'Changing the mood'. *HCIMA Reference Book 1985/86:* 349-350.

'How to grow and yet stay small'

In the early days of Catering & Allied, the company's thinking about entering into strategic alliances was focused on gearing up through partnerships to provide a superior service to clients. Through such alliances, the company achieved the flexibility to work with appropriate specialists outside the company and to benefit from the innovative synergy this offered.

Only later on did the company realize that the strategic alliance concept could offer other benefits. One of these was to help it meet the challenge of how to retain the advantages of smallness while at the same time growing the business. As Verstringhe put it: 'how to grow and stay small'. Many of its clients were asking Catering & Allied to stay small, for fear that a larger company would lose its particular style, attention to detail and above all the close personal contact with them. Yet growth was the natural consequence of succeeding in the marketplace.

The use of external specialists offered one way to achieve this aim. The first step came in the area of financial and company secretarial work. In 1975 Verstringhe had been introduced by his solicitor to Keith Moore, a senior partner of Smee Moore & Company, later Arnold Hill & Company. The reason for this introduction was that Catering & Allied's 10-year business and investment plan – the grey book as it was called – needed in the opinion of the solicitor to have its financial viability verified. From this initial meeting with Moore a working relationship developed. Moore was invited by the shareholders in November 1975 to carry out company secretarial activities in order to ensure that all the company's legal, administrative and fiscal affairs were conducted in a professional and efficient manner from the outset. It soon became apparent that Moore's experience was also invaluable in acting as company financial advisor in matters such as taxation, drawing up of the accounts, and keeping minutes of the board meetings. In 1981, Keith Moore was appointed Company Secretary to the board of Catering & Allied International. In this way, he was the first strategic alliance partner to become a formal member of the company. His contribution to the company evolved and he played a major role in setting up the Employee Share Scheme and the Employee Share Trust, and in negotiating the partnerships with Quality Catering Partners and later Elior.

By the end of the 1970s, working in partnership with outside specialists had become an established methodology at Catering & Allied. In 1981 the company decided to introduce computerization as a way of avoiding having to recruit junior and unskilled staff to cope with an increasing volume of paperwork. It preferred instead to upgrade the skills of its existing team and increase their remuneration. With these considerations in mind, advice was sought from Harry Sharpe who was head of the McAlpine Administration and Computer Centre in Hemel Hempstead. His advice was invaluable. He gave the management confidence to invest in a Wang computer, explained the separate role a software company can play, how to brief it, and how to verify that the external specialist had taken on board the company's precise requirements. This was the first time that a client company, McAlpine, played a role in the Catering & Allied strategic alliance concept.

The news spread that Catering & Allied had computerized its administrative system. As a result, the Industrial Society invited Verstringhe to speak at a seminar on two occasions on the use of computers in the catering business. Clearly, Catering & Allied was considered to be one of the first companies in its sector to achieve this technological advance.

However, by the beginning of the 1990s, further development of the company's information systems was required especially in accounting. To assist this process, it recruited David Pearce in September 1991 as Company Accountant. Pearce had specialist computer know-how and experience, and had recently qualified as a Certified Accountant. At that time, the accounting processes in Catering & Allied were predominantly manual. Although there were a reasonable number of PCs in the office, these were not networked and were of low specification. This lack of system integration meant that there was no integrated accounting system and that all of the core financial ledgers resided on individual PCs. It was very inconvenient and time consuming to share information. Management reporting was carried out using summary information compiled manually from various financial ledgers and client accounts. It was not possible to produce a balance sheet or complete management accounts on a monthly basis due to the system inefficiencies, and as a consequence management reports could only be reconciled fully at year-end.

The company's stress on individual attention to clients actually encouraged this lack of overall integration of accounting information. Due to the individual nature of each client contract in terms of industry, culture, contractual arrangements, and personalities involved, plus the varying catering arrangements in each site, each client account was very much unique. Reliance on Lotus 123 spreadsheets, the flexibility of which inhibited control, and the lack of integration between client accounts and financial ledgers perpetuated this uniqueness.

Clearly this approach suffered significantly from a lack of control and auditability, and incurred considerable duplication of effort. The first step in the search for a new integrated financial system was to visit Catering & Allied's sister company in The Netherlands, Holland Catering Specialisten, to learn from its experience. HCS had implemented a new accounting system, FIS2000, on the IBM mid-range AS400 platform. David Pearce became convinced that this IBM platform was suitable for whatever system Catering & Allied implemented because of its combination of performance, robustness, reliability and minimal support requirements. However, the FIS 2000 package was not suitable because of the problems of implementing a foreign language package with the many changes – cultural, discipline, skills and process – that would be required. It was therefore necessary to look for a solution from an outside software house. After investigation of five potential suppliers, the company decided on Pearce's recommendation to employ Lawson Software.

The process of working with Lawson's as a 'strategic alliance partner' bears strong similarities to the case of the Coopers and Lybrand development described earlier. Lawson's became immediately involved in the project, by arranging meetings with IBM to commence procurement of hardware and by recommending certain IBM business partners to provide technical support and training. A Catering & Allied steering group and project team were formed. The steering group consisted of two catering directors, a catering area manager, David Pearce, and a member from Lawson's. The project team consisted of the latter two persons plus two accounts clerks, a person working on bought ledger and one dealing with the sales ledger. The following sequence of developments was planned:

1. hardware procurement (AS400)
2. network setup (provided by SPACE Computer Systems)
3. technical training
4. software procurement and installation (Lawson)
5. application training: training the trainer
6. application definition workshops
7. application design
8. specification of software modifications
9. software development
10. software configuration
11. testing
12. parallel run on Chiltern area accounts
13. go-live Chiltern

There was a phased implementation, commencing with the Chiltern area and then continuing in sequence with London, international group accounts and de Blank Restaurants.

The reference to the Chiltern area denoted a further change in the company's boundaries that had been initiated with the establishment of Catering & Allied Services (Chiltern) Ltd in March 1989. This new affiliate, with Nigel Anker as Managing Director, was the first company in the group to venture beyond the self-imposed 35-mile radius of London. It was to focus on the area bounded on the East by the M11 as far as Cambridge and on the West by the M40 as far as Oxford. This area was chosen strategically because, as the location for many of Britain's fastest growing and most successful technologically-based manufacturing and service industries, it offered the best potential in terms of new business. It was agreed that Nigel Anker would have a major financial stake in the new company "on the understanding that you will not only continue with the successful expansion of the business but also very much that you will as a standard bearer carry Catering & Allied's philosophy and beliefs towards a new and exciting horizon. You know that besides the professional catering and business success that we endeavour to achieve, there is also that fundamental attitude to do it as a team and with a spirit that enables us to enhance all those ingredients that add value to and create a joie de vivre" (letter from Marc Verstringhe to Nigel Anker, 1 February 1989).

When the Government introduced new stringent food hygiene and health and safety legislation in the early 1990s, it seemed quite natural by then to seek the participation of external specialists to ensure compliance with them. The company invited Derek Gardner to help. Gardner had set up his own consulting business, Hygiene Impact, having previously been an environmental health officer in local government. His role on a strategic alliance basis with Catering & Allied involved the evaluation of its needs and the training of the people involved – including the board of directors – in understanding the new regulations and the legal implications of their implementation. The programme presented by Gardner was well received. The board asked that a manual be compiled to ensure that there was no equivocation in how the regulations were applied. This gave rise to the first and only manual that Catering & Allied ever had.

At the same time, employment laws and regulations were becoming more complicated. The company did not have a personnel manager, let alone a personnel department, and it set its face against introducing one. As a result, a decision was taken to once again approach an outside specialist to advise and guide all concerned in the company on matters relating to employment law and personnel procedures. Mike Duffay was engaged in this capacity.

By the late 1980s, the benefits achieved by recruiting and involving a team of outside specialists had become apparent to Catering & Allied's management. The company had from the outset worked with specialists in finance, taxation and related matters. It extended this 'strategic alliance' principle to working with external specialists in design, marketing, health and safety, human resources, purchasing and vending. The policy permitted access to the best design and technical resources, as with Coopers and Lybrand contract.

The value of this policy lay not only in the assistance such specialists provided. Equally, it enabled a flexible use of specialist services as and when required without incurring the overhead of in-house employment. As Verstringhe explained in an address to the Joint Hospitality Industry Congress in 1994, 'it means no empire building, the specialists need no office, no telephone or secretary – so besides engaging know how it is also very cost-effective'. Chapter Two presented the table drawn up by the company to illustrate the comparison in cost between tasks and responsibilities being carried out in-house and outsourcing them. The additional 7% contribution to profits that arose from outsourcing was reinvested so as to enable new talents to be recruited to the team some six to nine months before they were actually needed. In this way they could be inducted and made familiar with the Catering & Allied culture and philosophy of doing things.

A graphic drawn up by the company represents its 'strategic alliance' concept on the following page.

It is interesting to note that in one instance, that of payroll, the principle of outsourcing was reversed, although a strategic alliance partner assisted in the implementation of this change. A payroll bureau had been used for payroll processing. Within the company, there was just a small payroll department of two persons. Since they manually entered data into the system, all the bureau was effectively doing was simply to process the payroll on the company's behalf. This arrangement was unsatisfactory because it involved a lengthy turnaround of payroll reports which were also inflexible in structure, required very tight processing deadlines, created less accurate payroll results due to early cut-off of data transmission, and development rates were costly. At the same time, a single user PC personnel system (PWA) had been implemented to improve training, rewards, discipline and employment history records. However, a single individual outside of the payroll department

Strategic
Alliance

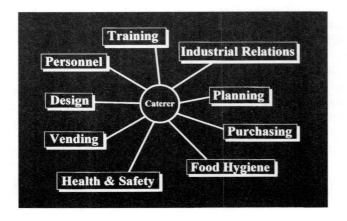

operated this system, which was not integrated in any way with the payroll bureau systems and became laborious to maintain.

The implementation of the Lawson accounting and finance system with the availability of spare processing power on the IBM AS400, presented Catering & Allied with an opportunity to bring payroll back in-house. The objective of integrating the payroll and personnel information systems was agreed, subject to the following criteria:

1. the new system must run on the AS400 platform with an option to switch platforms without penalties

2. it must integrate payroll and personnel systems

3. the annual revenue cost must not exceed the bureau costs

4. the personnel function would be incorporated into the payroll department

A similar process to that employed successfully in the Lawson project was followed in this one, with very similar results. A company called Coggon, now renamed Prolog, was quickly identified as being the best fit for the above criteria and in terms of functionality. It became Catering & Allied's 'alliance' partner for the project.

Joint ventures with other catering companies

The aim of staying small while growing also informed Catering & Allied's formation of joint ventures with other catering companies. Such ventures could capitalize on complementary strengths and experiences, while also offering administrative, purchasing and other economies.

The first instance occurred in 1987 with the formation of a joint venture with Justin de Blank. For some time, Catering & Allied had been purchasing fine foods and special bread from the Justin de Blank shop in Elizabeth Street. When John Carter, a former Sutcliffe catering accountant joined the Justin de Blank Company, he soon initiated a meeting with Verstringhe and Cuthbert. At the time, they were not aware that de Blank fine foods also operated a number of High Street restaurants, nor that it provided the catering for the National Gallery. On visiting the latter it was clear that the style of food, service and ambiance was far superior to the standard generally available in museums.

The opportunity to form a partnership presented itself when both Justin de Blank and Catering & Allied were invited to tender for the catering at the British Museum. The project involved both staff catering for 1000 meals a day and the public restaurant. Justin de Blank had no experience of staff catering, whereas Catering & Allied was attracted by having seen what could be achieved in museum catering at the Museum of Modern Art in New York. The new style of museum catering offered an exciting avenue for growth consistent with the company's quality image.

To go into partnership with Justin de Blank offered Catering & Allied an opportunity to enter what was for the company a new niche market segment, without jeopardizing its own distinct brand and specialization. It would also permit the transfer of know-how and experience. It involved investment into a new stand-alone company called Catering & Allied/Justin de Blank, trading as de Blank Restaurants. When the company was awarded the British Museum contract, John Houston contacted Digby Trout, whom he had met on a previous occasion, and invited him to join the new venture.

Trout was appointed as the General Manager of de Blank Restaurants. The business grew steadily, securing some of the most prestigious locations in the country such as the Science Museum, Heals Restaurant, the Orangery at Royal Kensington Palace, the Barbican, the Ashmolean in Oxford, and the Tower of London. In due course, Trout became Managing Director of the company.

The two partner companies, however, had different patterns of working. Justin de Blank made a proposal to buy out the other 50% of the company. Catering & Allied countered with its own bid, which was accepted. Nevertheless, Catering & Allied's core business was also expanding rapidly at the time and it would therefore have stretched its managerial capacities to run de Blank Restaurants on its own. Digby Trout had expressed an interest for a management buy-in of the company and his proposal was therefore accepted.

The new company, called Digby Trout Restaurants, was established in 1992 with Trout having 80% of the shares and Catering & Allied 20%. To ease the financial burden on Trout, it was agreed to spread the payment over a period of three years. The advantages of sharing an office, the pooling of back office services through the computerization programme, shared purchasing and the exchange of know how and best practice continued to provide added value to both companies in financial as well as operational terms. Upon Justin de Blank's retirement, Verstringhe was invited to become the Chairman of Digby Trout Restaurants. The other directors were Digby Trout, Robyn Lines (a founder member) and Mike Gilpin. At the time of going to print, the turnover of the business had reached £14 million.

Other issues motivated the establishment of a more extensive partnership - with other European catering companies. One was concern about how to secure the long-term future for Catering & Allied beyond the retirement of its founders. Another was the need to ensure that the company could continue to compete with global players such as Compass, Sodexho, Marriott and Aramark.

In January 1994, Catering & Allied therefore formed an alliance called the Quality Catering Partners, a company registered and domiciled in Zurich. It brought together four organizations in a relationship that was intended to change the image of catering in Europe. The companies were Partena Cater in Sweden and Norway, SV-Service in Switzerland and Germany, Holland Catering Specialisten in The Netherlands, and Catering & Allied in Britain. The objective was to share expertise while remaining quite independent companies. Expertise could beneficially be pooled in areas such as purchasing, design and planning, training and health and safety. By sharing their international expertise, the partners could offer benefits to their clients in the countries where they operated.

The four companies were aware that they also shared a common philosophy, which offered the basis for a pooling of their identities within a larger concept. This common philosophy was stated in its brochure as follows:

We have many things in common. We relate to our clients' culture and strategy; we do not seek to standardize the restaurants but rather create a quality image specifically for the client; our most senior executives in our companies are fully involved in every part of the business and we are all totally committed to providing the highest standards of service and quality.

The total consistency of this statement with the distinctive approach that Catering & Allied had developed over the previous twenty years is evident.

Into Europe: Catering & Allied in context

In an atmosphere of growing Europeanization/globalization throughout industry as a whole, the year 1995 in particular saw a flurry of link ups between major UK based contract caterers and Continental companies.

In January of that year, Gardner Merchant, the leading UK contractor with an annual turnover of £500m and a 27% share of the market by value (Key Note 1996) entered into strategic alliance with Sodexho, the leisure and catering company founded in Marseilles by Pierre Bellon in 1966 and which, in just under 30 years of trading, had gained representation in 60 countries worldwide including Africa, the Middle East, North and South America and Eastern Europe (Sodexho Corporate Fact File 2000). Its total sales in the year to 31 August 1995 of £18.3 bn included around £1.8bn in respect of its contract catering activities of which Gardner Merchant was now a critical part (Key Note 1996; *Sunday Times*, 15 January 1995).

Under the heading 'A successful alliance', an advertisement run by Sodexho head office in the *Financial Times* of 4 January 1996 referred to the alliance with Gardner Merchant as 'the year's most important event ... which transformed Sodexho into the world's largest food services group'. Although Garry Hawkes, who led the management buyout of Gardner Merchant from Forte in 1992, had resisted previous takeover attempts of the company by Compass and then Granada, the deal with Sodexho enabled him to retain his position as CEO of Gardner Merchant, which continued to operate under this name, as well as becoming Directeur Général of Sodexho. This situation obtained for five years until Hawkes resigned in protest at the UK board decision to change the Gardner Merchant name to Sodexho in February 2000 (*Caterer & Hotelkeeper*, 10 February 2000; 2 March 2000).

In July 1995, Compass Group became the largest contract caterer worldwide through its acquisition of the food services management company Eurest from the French group Accor. Annual turnover worldwide leapt to £2.9 bn (Key Note 1996), with £1.5 bn accounted for by the business and industry operation (*Caterer & Hotelkeeper*, 15 February 1996). The company responsible for this area of service delivery, trading as Compass Services, took the name Eurest just seven months after the takeover, in February 1996. This is an interesting scenario when compared with the Gardner Merchant/Sodexho situation, the wider implications of which are further discussed in Chapter Eight.

A third significant association between a UK based contract caterer and French company was agreed in April 1995 between Catering & Allied and Elior. At the time, Elior was the largest contract caterer in France, with a total turnover of £190m on operations in France, Spain and the UK, while Catering & Allied had a turnover of £50m on 215 contracts in London and The Netherlands (*Caterer & Hotelkeeper*, 27 April 1995). The agreement took the form of a strategic alliance, involving the creation of a holding company, Eurocater, owned 50% by the three founders of Catering & Allied – Cuthbert, Koops and Verstringhe – and 50% by Elior. Initially, each of the three founders contributed 191,000 Catering & Allied shares to Eurocater, effectively giving Elior a 27% holding in Catering & Allied. Under the terms of the deal, a series of cash injections by Elior into Catering & Allied would, as further shares became available, ultimately increase the Eurocater interest in Catering & Allied to a majority holding by the year 2000.

The motivation for this agreement, described by Verstringhe in his 1995 chairman's report as a 'partenariat', was to ensure continuity of the Catering & Allied core values and independence while protecting the company from other predators and enhancing competitive advantage through increased resources in terms of know-how, experience, purchasing, information technology and marketing. Also encouraging was the successful relationship, now in its fifth year, between Elior and its first UK acquisition, the London-based executive dining and contract catering group High Table.

In 1998, Holland Catering, the Dutch company of Catering & Allied, was brought together with Restoplan and Le Grand Bernard – the Dutch businesses of Elior – as Elior Nederland, then 49% owned by Catering & Allied and 51% by the Elior group, with Koops as CEO. This was a successful merger of interests which yet maintained the separate brand images of the constituent companies; final consolidation came in May 1999, when High Table, Elior Nederland and Catering & Allied were brought together under the Eurocater umbrella (cf Baker 1999; Eurocater Offer to Purchase, 2 July 1999). Under the terms of this latter deal, Eurocater became a full subsidiary of the Elior group, which by that time owned 80% of the Eurocater shares and Catering & Allied shareholders the remaining 20%. Verstringhe described the deal at the time as effectively enabling Catering & Allied to invest its assets without having to sell its shares, and to share ownership in Elior through the Eurocater subsidiary, all part of the fundamental strategy of 'continuing to grow while staying small' (cf Baker 1999).

In July 1999, a Recommended Offer to Purchase was sent to all shareholders of Catering and Allied (International) Ltd, in which Eurocater plc offered to acquire the whole of the issued share capital of the company not already in its ownership. Integral to the Offer was the grant of put and call options by and in favour of Elior UK over the Eurocater shares to be issued as part consideration. The right to call for the transfer of such Eurocater shares was also granted to Elior, at any time after 1 January 2003. In his letter of recommendation of the Offer, Verstringhe noted, *inter alia*, that on its completion he would cease to be a full time employee of Catering & Allied, although he would remain as co-chair of Eurocater with the co-founder and co-chairman of Elior, Robert Zolade, until 31 December 2004. Kit Cuthbert had already retired from the board and Keith Moore and Bob Foster would also be standing down, after a combined service to the company of nearly 39 years.

The question such a scenario raises is, how to ensure the continuation of company ethos and principles, especially in a situation of merger or acquisition, when the founders, directors and guardians of those principles retire? Various factors impact on this, including the nature of the acquisition, its implications for organizational identity, and how intangible assets such as reputational capital (cf Fombrun 1996) are subsequently managed.

In their seminal work on managing acquisitions, Haspeslagh and Jemison (1991) identify three main acquisitive processes:

- Absorbing the other firm
- Preserving what you bought
- Amalgamating the two organizations

The situation with Catering & Allied can be seen to have illustrated elements of all three strategies, although the company was ultimately absorbed following the retirement of Verstringhe in 1999. Haspeslagh and Jemison (ibid: 189) describe absorption as an 'integration approach' which tends to occur where there is 'high interdependence between the firms and there is less concern about maintaining the autonomy of the acquired .. firm' – at least, that is, from the perspective of the acquirer. Growth through mergers and acquisitions is a salient feature of the food services industry and raises a number of issues, including those of autonomy and identity, that are further discussed in Chapter Eight.

References

Baker, J (1999). 'Growing small'. *Caterer & Hotelkeeper*, 10 June: 28-29

Bernoth, A (1995). 'Gardner serves up a cordon bleu deal'. *The Sunday Times*, 15 January: 2.5

Caterer & Hotelkeeper, 2 March 2000

Caterer & Hotelkeeper, 10 February 2000

Caterer & Hotelkeeper, 15 February 1996

Caterer & Hotelkeeper, 27 April 1995

Child, J (2001). 'Trust: The fundamental bond in global collaboration'. *Organizational Dynamics*, 29/4: 274-288.

Child, J and D Faulkner (1998). *Strategies of Co-operation*. Oxford: Oxford University Press.

Child, J and S Rodrigues (2003). 'Social identity and organizational learning'. In M Easterby-Smith and M A Lyles (eds) *Handbook of Organizational Learning*. Oxford: Blackwell (forthcoming)

Contractor, F J and P Lorange (1988). 'Why should firms cooperate? The strategy and economics basis for cooperative ventures'. In F J Contractor.and P Lorange (eds) *Co-operative Strategies in International Business*. New York: Lexington Books, 3-28

Devanna, M A and N Tichy (1990). 'Creating the competitive organization of the 21st century: The boundaryless corporation'. *Human Resource Management*, 29/4: 455-471

Edmondson, A (1999). 'Psychological safety and learning behavior in work teams'. *Administrative Science Quarterly*, 44/2: 350-383

Eurocater Offer to Purchase, 2 July 1999

Faulkner, D and M de Rond (2000). 'Perspectives on cooperative strategy'. In D Faulkner and M de Rond (eds) *Cooperative Strategy: Economic, Business and Organizational Issues*. Oxford: Oxford University Press, 3-39

The Financial Times, 4 January 1996

Fombrun, C J (1996). *Reputation*. Boston: Harvard Business School Press

Hamel, G and C-K Prahalad (1994). *Competing for the Future*. Boston, MA: Harvard Business School Press

Haspeslagh, P C and D B Jemison (1991). *Managing acquisitions: Creating value through corporate renewal*. New York: The Free Press

Ratcliffe, Z (ed) (1996). *Contract catering: 1996 market report*. 9th edition. Hampton: Key Note

Sodexho Corporate Fact File, March 2000

The Sunday Times, 15 January 1995

Wellins, R S, W C Byham and G R Dixon (1994). *Inside Teams: How 20 World-Class Organizations are Winning Through Teamwork*. San Francisco: Jossey-Bass

Chapter Seven

Learning and Knowledge Management

The issue of learning in organizations has become increasingly significant within the management literature, for reasons that are perhaps most succinctly summarized by Stata (1989: 64) in his perception of organizational learning as 'the principal process by which management innovation occurs' and that 'the rate at which individuals and organizations learn may become the only sustainable competitive advantage'.

This is a particularly cogent perspective for our consideration of Catering & Allied as a learning organization, especially if we consider the nature of their service provision implicit in which is the continuous application of knowledge concerning client desires, as discussed in earlier chapters of this book. The 'rate' at which the learning takes place – and is applied – is significant in service delivery, as pointed up by Bob Cotton, Chief Executive Officer of the British Hospitality Association, in his observation that contract catering is essentially a responsive industry, responding '*precisely*' to what is required: 'the right specification, at the right price, delivered in the right way ... very precisely, and probably just exceeding, client expectation'. For the client, this is what constitutes a 'top quality product', and key to the development of such service, in which 'what the caterer can do for the client, and how, are paramount', are 'listening, and understanding, and interpreting', all of which contribute to the assessment of a client which, for Cotton, is 'a skill that should not be underestimated'.

The above processes of developing competitive advantage clearly involve an element of learning, but what is the nature of 'learning'? It is a concept that is difficult to define *per se* but, through reformulating Argyris and Schön's query 'What is an organization that it may learn?' (1978: 9), we can contextualize it by asking 'What is learning that an organization might achieve it?'. One influential perspective is that of Cyert and March (1963, 1992) who, in their seminal work on a behavioural theory of the firm, see it in terms of adaptive behaviour. Certainly, a degree of learning is involved where adaptation leads to beneficial change, i.e. 'the type of change that leads to an improved fit between an organization and environment or other contingencies' (Child and Heavens 2001: 308/309).

Learning refers to both process and outcome (Child and Heavens 2001); as process, it might include, *inter alia*, the application of extant knowledge to a new situation and the ongoing development of new knowledge, with outcome being seen, for example, in the acquisition of a new competence. From this, it is clear that learning and innovation – the creation or introduction of something new – are closely linked, and it is also interesting in this regard to consider the work by Kirton (1994) on adaption-innovation, axiomatic to which is that all creativity occurs within structure and which places adaptors and innovators at opposite ends of a continuum. It is possible for us to see learning as the dynamic that drives this continuum from adaption through to innovation, and from innovative outcome through to further adaption.

When relating these points to the case of Catering & Allied, it is useful to return to the point of company set up and the tacit knowledge available to the nascent enterprise through the input of the founding executive. Huber (1991: 91) refers to this as 'inherited knowledge', observing that 'organizations do not begin their lives with clean slates. The individuals ... that create new organizations have knowledge about the new organization's initial environment and about the processes the organization can use to carry out its creator's intentions'. The picture is further developed through the observation by Pavitt (1991: 42) that 'tacit knowledge obtained through experience' is of 'central importance' to innovating firms, and we have earlier noted this factor – and the ability to disseminate such knowledge - as rendering individuals key within Catering & Allied.

The critical role of individuals in organizational learning is pointed up by authors such as Kim (1993: 37) who notes that 'organizations ultimately learn via their individual members', although he also implies that such learning may not be dependent on any one individual: 'organizations can learn independent of a specific individual but not independent of all individuals'. At the start up of a company in particular, however, the contribution of the founder members is key; not only because of the tacit knowledge they invest in the new enterprise but also because the innovative contextualization of this knowledge uniquely shapes the ensuing learning process. As Huber (1991: 91) notes, the time interval between the conception of a new organization and its 'birth event' (e.g. incorporation) is one in which the organization's founders seek to acquire additional knowledge, 'searching to learn on behalf of the organization-to-be', a search which is shaped by its inherited knowledge.

In the case of Catering & Allied, the competences available to the company through its founders at set up were fundamental to its identification and realization of market niche, resulting in an innovative approach to contract catering through the application of extant knowledge in a new context; i.e. hotelier/restaurateur expertise and philosophy applied to an industrial canteen situation. As earlier noted, the innovative recontextualization of knowledge is one way in which the learning process may be initiated both within and across organizational boundaries.

In a service context in particular, this learning dynamic can be cyclical; not only may the client learn from the contractor, there is also the potential as noted by Sivula et al (1997: 121) for 'client alliances (to) provide an important way to build the competences of the service firm' and enable the development of its knowledge base. This learning perspective on, specifically, *client* alliances is of particular significance for this chapter as, although alliances are recognized in the literature as creating a context for learning, they are more usually addressed from the perspective of international joint ventures (cf Inkpen 1996; Lyles 2001), strategic alliances (Child 2001; Hamel 1991) and other transnational inter-firm relationships (Lipparini and Fratocchi 1999).

Leadership and learning

Although structures and contexts conducive to learning can be created, these are, in themselves, not sufficient to ensure that the learning potential of an organization is realized. The process has to be facilitated by individuals within the organization for, as Corrigan (1999: 31) observes, 'as an individual you learn and change. Structures don't'. Leadership is an important agency for organizational learning; for example, the issue of individual responsibility for organizational learning is frequently addressed from the perspective of management-as-leader; for example, Senge (1990) states that 'leaders in learning organizations are responsible for *building organizations* where people are continually expanding their capabilities to shape their future – that is, leaders are responsible for learning' (p 9) and, though he acknowledges that leadership skills should be widely distributed throughout an organization, he explicitly addresses the issue of 'top managers ... moving toward learning organizations' (p 20). Farkas et al (1995) identify five approaches by 'top' leadership to add value to their companies, one of which is *'explicitly* (to) *spread a specific expertise* between business units' (p 77), while von Krogh et al (2000: 71/72) propose a framework for the strategic assessment of knowledge as 'top management rarely focuses on the strategic role of knowledge or the importance of knowledge creation initiatives'. Argyris (2000: 219) states categorically that 'to be successful, a program to create a learning organization must begin at the top'.

Leadership is often required in order to create the conditions for learning by breaking the mould of embedded thinking and practice. Some leadership of the organizational learning process itself is necessary for it to be directed towards clear goals, coordinated, informed by open channels of communication and, not least, adequately supported with resources. However, this implies a degree of top-down direction, which it may not be easy to reconcile with the autonomy and open-mindedness commonly regarded as requisites for creative learning. Indeed, the pressures for change and reform emanating from learning within an organization can easily be interpreted as a challenge to its senior leadership. The inherent tension between leadership and devolved autonomy can therefore be problematic for organizational learning.

The potential contribution of leadership to organizational learning encompasses a number of roles. The most fundamental is that of establishing a culture conducive to organizational learning. Sometimes it is necessary to transform the embedded legacy of the past from being a barrier to an asset. In other circumstances, as with Catering & Allied, a culture conducive to learning was established at the outset by a small cohesive group of leaders who in setting up on their own had already developed a clear set of values.

The communication of a clear and strong vision from the top can often break down the barriers to learning that might otherwise exist within a company. If a barrier proves insuperable, however, it may have to be destroyed. Radical moves away from embedded organizational cultural webs, sometimes termed 'frame-breaking' changes or 'transformations', have to be led from the top. Jack Welch performed this role at the General Electric Company. The other side of the coin is that a conservative organizational leader, who clings to an established set of policies and practices, insulating himself or herself against changing realities, can have the power to prevent an organization from learning and adapting. It is therefore not surprising that radical changes and corporate turnarounds usually require the bringing in of new senior managers from outside, as well as the direct involvement of executives in all aspects of the process (Grinyer et al 1988).

Radical change presents the most dramatic connection between organizational leadership and learning, but the culture that it aims to create has also to be sustained on a more everyday basis. Tensions can arise between the element of control within managerial leadership and the degree of autonomy that is a further condition for effective learning within organizations. Therefore, a second leadership role in promoting organizational learning is to establish a modus operandi that permits the autonomy needed to encourage the creation of insight and new knowledge, within a sense of collective effort that is directed towards the development of the organization as a whole.

A third leadership role in respect of organizational learning is to foster the channels of communication and relationships across a firm's internal and external organizational boundaries that are key to the learning process. The first channel is between higher management and other groups within an organization. There is a division of function here in that higher management will normally be concerned with strategic knowledge, while other groups will work more on organizational and technical knowledge. Each area of knowledge needs to be informed by the others. In particular, the degree of support that higher management gives to learning activities and systems at lower levels of an organization can have a major impact on their effectiveness.

The second channel involves the integration of knowledge contributions between different specialties and units within an organization. As Catering & Allied became more diversified in its geographical coverage and number of affiliates focusing on specialized segments of the market, so it perceived the need to devote increasing attention to ensuring that the experience of its different units was adequately shared. Cross-unit integration is a requirement for organizational learning and the effective operation of knowledge databases.

The third channel promotes flows of information and knowledge across the boundaries of an organization through communication with, and intelligence from, other organizations and groups including customers, suppliers, network partners, competitors, and research institutes. Cross-organizational knowledge flows can occur at any level of an organization, though flows relevant to strategic learning tend to be concentrated at the upper levels and those relevant to organizational and technical learning lower down.

For Verstringhe, leadership means getting involved in order to realize the values on which Catering & Allied had been founded. His preferred style is 'virtual leadership' (Kanter 1989), which he describes as 'giving support to people on the spot who make things happen' – and in respect of learning, 'an involvement [which extends] beyond the parameters of one's immediate business' (Sutton 1994).

This approach to learning appreciates the value of delegated initiative based on the superior local knowledge that people close to the action inevitably have. It is also appropriate to the fast-moving conditions under which business operates today. The environment that companies, Catering & Allied included, face nowadays is characterized by increasing discontinuity and turbulence. This makes it even less tenable than previously for top management to hold or even understand all of the information relevant to adapting their organization to these changing conditions. While it is the role of senior management to make sure that its organization has an appropriate sense of long-term direction, organizational learning also requires a degree of cognitive and behavioural initiative on the part of organizational members who are in closer touch with relevant events and developments. The challenge for leadership in facilitating organizational learning therefore lies in maintaining a judicious combination of both control, in the form of guidance and back up, and the autonomy required to motivate knowledge generators and encourage the free flow of information.

The capacity of a company to learn, and consequently to adapt, is therefore enhanced through virtual leadership. It is important to realize that this does not mean 'faceless leadership'. Far from it; nobody could call Verstringhe 'faceless'. The concept, and the way it was practiced in Catering & Allied, focuses the top managers' attention onto what they alone are capable of doing. It grants them the role of articulating a vision and identity for their company based on a set of coherent underlying values. The framework of shared understanding provided by this corporate vision and identity then allows for operational leadership with a light touch. Rather than having to be closely monitored, the members of the company can be guided by a culture that they freely accept and which leaves them free to decide on its best application in the light of the changing circumstances they directly experience. This localization of operational discretion engages people more actively with clients, suppliers and other external parties, which makes them into much more effective agents for importing new relevant information into the company's learning process.

Leadership for learning also denotes the willingness to allocate material as well as moral resources in support. Time is an especially significant resource because learning requires a double time investment. The time that is taken up by personnel learning new practices, and in standing back from a situation in order to assimilate new information, is also time that is 'lost' to the organization while learners step out of their usual roles and routines in order to accomplish the learning.

This concept of leadership therefore provides organizational learning with direction sufficient to ensure that it is regarded as significant and thus adequately supported, while also allowing sufficient autonomy to the process so that it is capable of producing new insights. For instance, Catering & Allied saved considerable costs in its purchasing by reducing the range of its suppliers without sacrificing food quality when its managing director set such saving as a target but left it to teams of chefs, restaurant managers and other staff with operational knowledge to decide which suppliers the company should retain.

There is, however, increasing recognition of the actions and interactions within and across organizational levels and boundaries in the process of knowledge creation (Nonaka et al 2001; Nonaka and Takeuchi 1995) and the need for 'learning leaders at *all* levels, from the chief executive to the leaders of shop-floor groups' to facilitate this (Sadler 2001: 426). Communications are fundamental to the process, and a significant leadership role specific to organizational learning is to foster the three main channels of communication and relationships, namely those between 1) higher management and other, more specialized groups within an organization; 2) different specialties within an organization; and 3) the organization and other groups or bodies, including customers, suppliers, network partners, competitors, and research institutes, with the potential for knowledge flow at any level (Child and Heavens 2001: 313).

In considering the issues of leadership and learning in respect of Catering & Allied, it is important to remember the two guiding and driving principles of the company: total commitment to client satisfaction, and people working with, not for. Realizing these aims involved a unique structure and strategy, as discussed in earlier chapters, with the devolution of authority to unit level in the context of a supportive yet flexible management framework. From the perspective of leadership *per se*, it is interesting to consider the point by Peters and Waterman (1982: 82) concerning the various factors that constitute this function, prominent amongst which is 'building a loyal team at the top that speaks more or less with one voice'. This certainly describes the key team assembled by Marc Verstringhe at the birth of the company; Sarah Banner, Kit Cuthbert, Vi Haire and Jop Koops all remained with the company until retirement. The fact that they 'spoke with one voice' had much to do with their shared,

Sutcliffe history, and the experience of working with one another that reached back, in the case of Verstringhe and Cuthbert, nearly 15 years prior to the incorporation of Catering & Allied. They subscribed to the same values that underpinned and informed the creative processes of the company, in the manner of Selznick's observation of nearly 50 years ago that the creative leader is 'primarily an expert in the promotion and protection of values' (1957: 153).

Learning through partnerships

Access to information outside a firm's boundaries, and knowledge creation through collaboration with other firms, are becoming increasingly important. This is particularly true in sectors such as bio-technology which have a complex and expanding knowledge base and where sources of expertise are widely dispersed (Powell et al. 1996). The permeability of firms' boundaries, and provisions for transferring information across them, therefore have considerable consequences for organizational learning. The effective transfer of information and knowledge into a firm depends on the effectiveness of this process.

It is vital for a firm's capacity to innovate and to learn in other ways that it receives relevant new information from its external environment. This information can relate to all levels of organizational activity: strategic, organizational and technical. Top management through its external connections, via membership of other companies' boards, trade associations, governmental working parties, and the like, can be an important conduit for the input of information relevant to strategic learning. At the technical level, which has been the focus for research on innovation, relevant specialists and R&D project teams must maintain effective connections with external sources of technical information such as universities and research institutes.

The inputs to a firm's learning process that flow across its boundaries can vary from ill-structured and scattered items of news to highly codified sets of knowledge. It is generally assumed that the less codified and more tacit the knowledge, the more difficult it will be for the receiving organization to make sense of it, even if it gains access to it in the first place. One

133

of the reasons why firms are encouraged to work closely in joint ventures or other forms of collaboration is that this enhances their opportunity to access and make use of the tacit, uncodified knowledge held by, and embedded within, their partners. The alternative is to recruit personnel from the other organization(s) who hold such knowledge, and then to graft them onto the 'home' system.

Firms are increasingly forming alliances with the specific intention of acquiring new knowledge and know-how. Even when alliances are formed for reasons other than learning and knowledge acquisition, such acquisition can be a desirable by-product of their collaboration. Alliances are hybrid arrangements for they combine the strategic objectives and cultures of the partner organizations. When they are achieved through the establishment of a new joint venture, alliances may also have to combine elements of the partners' management structures and systems. The hybrid nature of alliances has a number of implications for the possibilities of learning through them. A positive feature is that the complementary expertise and knowledge brought to an alliance by partners can promote learning both through transfer and through the dynamic synergy that may be stimulated by the coming together of experts from different corporate, and perhaps national, backgrounds. Alliances between comparatively small, research-intensive biotechnology firms and rather large pharmaceutical companies with expertise in development, production, and marketing serve as one example. A problematic feature lies in the barriers to knowledge-sharing between alliance partners, barriers that can arise for a number of reasons. The underlying relationship between the partners may remain fundamentally competitive. It may prove difficult to reconcile the different corporate or social identities of their staff. The members of an organization may assume that they have nothing to learn from their partners. Companies may not have the experience or capacity to acquire and absorb the knowledge available from their alliance partners.

Lindholm (1997) categorizes three different processes through which learning can take place in joint ventures. The first is the *transfer of knowledge* by the partners to the joint venture, much of it in the form of technology transfer. A similar transfer of knowledge may take place directly between partners who collaborate by means other than setting up a separate joint venture. This form of transfer involves the movement of existing technology, knowledge, or management practice into an organizational setting for which such transfer represents a new knowledge input. The second learning process is different because it involves the creation of *new* knowledge, or at least a *substantial transformation* of existing knowledge, within the ambit of the cooperative venture. This process implies that mutual learning occurs through a constructive integration of the different inputs offered by the partners and their members. This type of learning is qualitatively different from learning through knowledge transfer, and its realization presents a correspondingly greater challenge. It is, nevertheless, one of the potential prizes of cooperation between organizations that can offer one another valuable complementary knowledge. The third learning process, which Lindholm calls 'harvesting' (*ibid*:141), involves the retrieval of knowledge that has been generated in the joint venture or other collaborative unit and its internalization within the parent firms so that they can use it in other areas of operation. These processes indicate that strategic alliances can provide a means to acquire or generate knowledge that might otherwise not be available. Alliances can also be an important vehicle for the incorporation of new knowledge into practice, particularly through the medium of joint ventures or cross-partner teams that work on the necessary adaptation and application of knowledge drawn from the partners.

Business schools and academic links

In 1966, on a visit to America organized by the HCI (now HCIMA), Verstringhe met with Dean Beck of the Cornell Hotel and Catering University. This meeting was to have a profound effect on the approach to business by Sutcliffe as mediated by Verstringhe who was, at this time, London area manager. Beck advised him to invest in skilling up staff and management, supporting them with the necessary equipment and foodstuffs to satisfy customer requirements. This was in contrast to the prevailing trend of the time, at which the leading catering companies were concentrating on the provision of frozen or centrally prepared cook-chill meals – for example, Unilever's 'Top Tray' and Mars' 'Four Square' systems - an approach which saved on space and skilled labour costs but denied to the customer a choice of fresh food.

Verstringhe was keen to apply the insights and philosophy of Beck and was given the opportunity when Honeywell Controls, a large US company with offices in London, became dissatisfied with the Four Square system and awarded their catering contract to Sutcliffe. The approach developed for Honeywell became known as the combo system, and was based on the following criteria:

- Freshly cooked main meals skilfully blended with a combination of frozen foods and convenience foods (ready peeled potatoes, washed vegetables and salads, etc

- Automatic vending machines as required

- Bussing system (the diner returns his/her own tray)

- The use of disposables for hors d'oeuvres, sweets and drinks whilst still using china plates for the main meal, thus saving on washing up, space and labour

- Introduction of free-flow serveries wherever possible, to improve the display of foods, maximize self-service and generally speed up the service to reduce queuing

There were several advantages to this approach. From the perspective of the customer, there was a wider menu offering real choice between freshly prepared dishes, while, for the caterer, it enabled flexibility in equipment and facilitated the purchase of foodstuffs in a wider market, enabling the best produce to be sourced at the best price. There were also space and cost saving benefits; it is important to remember that an essential part of achieving less labour intensive methods of providing a catering service is to eliminate many of the unskilled parts of jobs. This can be done – as advocated by Beck - through investment in skilling up management and staff through appropriate training and the provision of modern equipment and facilities. On average, the result is an increase in productivity of between 35% and 50%, and a reduction in cost of 30/40%.

Between 1968 – the year Verstringhe was appointed managing director of Sutcliffe London – and 1969, area business expanded by 54% largely as a result of the success of the combo system.

Handy (1990: 199) describes learning organizations as those 'which relish curiosity, questions and ideas, which allow time for experiment and reflection, which ... promote self-confidence' and thereby develop 'a competitive advantage which no-one can steal from them'. The combo system was certainly one such learning experiment, with a competitive advantage that extended beyond the UK into Europe.

The system was, in fact, fundamental to the expansion of Sutcliffe Catering in Continental Europe. In 1969, having established a company in The Netherlands as part of the ongoing business development programme, Verstringhe and his colleagues invited the then head of Shell Catering, John Shulten, to visit some of the Sutcliffe operations in London. This created the opportunity to demonstrate the benefits of the combo system and, following this visit, the company was invited to tender for a large complex to be built by Shell in Moerdijk. The tender document specified that 'a knowledge of the combo system would be an advantage' and, as no-one outside Sutcliffe knew what that was, its Dutch subsidiary was successful in gaining the contract.

Advanced Management Programme International (AMPI)

In 1972, following Verstringhe's appointment as group managing director of Sutcliffe Catering, he attended the Advanced Management Programme (AMP) being taught by Harvard Business School faculty at University College, Swansea. The Director of Programmes was Professor Harry Hansen, whose expertise in strategic planning and marketing management would have a profound and enduring influence on the business thinking of Verstringhe.

The programme was – and continues to be – concerned with overall direction of the business enterprise and the determination and implementation of corporate strategy in an increasingly international context. It is designed for senior executives and delivers its teaching over an intensive four (originally six) week period via lectures and some 60 actual business case studies. The programme, now housed at Templeton College, Oxford, has developed considerably since J Walter Thompson executive Denys Scott persuaded Harvard faculty to run a one-off, six week course at Durham University in 1964. At the time, as recalled by John Bolton, an MBA student of Harry Hansen and Chairman of Council and Founder Subscriber of the Foundation for Management Education, there was much controversy in Britain about the value of problem-oriented teaching, despite its proven track record in the United States. The course, however, was a success, and Bolton and Hansen were persuaded that this was an opportune time in Britain, where management education was still in its infancy, to pioneer the case study method of teaching in the context of a continuing management development programme. The AMPI educational trust was created in 1965 to administer and promote the new programme, the first of which Bolton had personally agreed to underwrite. He went on to chair the trust for 20 years, during which time it gave scholarships to academics and trades union officials to participate in the programme.

After Durham, the programme was held at the University of Bangor, then at Strathclyde, and subsequently for 16 years at Swansea University. In 1983, the AMPI trust handed the course over to Templeton College, University of Oxford, where demand has grown such that the Programme is now offered three times a year. Since the handover, the AMPI trust - to which Verstringhe succeeded as chair in 1985 - has concentrated on research, including the founding of the Hansen Research Fellowship in 1991, a year before Professor Hansen's death. The Fellowship was originally established within Emmanuel College, Cambridge because of its links with Harvard, being John Harvard's old college, and the founding that same year of the Judge Institute of Management at Cambridge University. The relationship with Cambridge has been further developed through the Centre for International Business and Management at the Judge Institute.

At the time of the handover, Hansen recalled the original decision to 'build the programme over time until it was secure in its reputation then pass it into the control of an eminent business school. At that time, control by the charitable foundation and the Americans would fade away'. What did not fade away, however, was the original focus on individual learning and development that continues central to the programme and remains a dynamic influence on its graduates. As Verstringhe recalls, a major legacy of the programme in general, and Harry Hansen in particular, was the perception of the opportunities that inhere in apparent problems. Hansen's philosophy was rooted in the challenge as raison d'être and, from a management perspective, points up the critical role of business education in enabling identification, interpretation and creative response to the challenges 'man lives on' and which 'he must find ... or ... retrogress into an aimless, drifting passivity. He stands before one today, if he has but the imagination and wit to see it'. For Hansen, the challenge was 'a managerial one: the marshalling, deployment, and use of resources, so that man can live a better and safer life, and a more self-fulfilling one'. The aim of management education was to enable this process; not to teach principles, 'because there are no principles of management', nor the theory of management 'for there is no such theory'; rather, 'the basic aim of business education is to develop men (sic) to lead business enterprises' (Hansen 1970: 1, 2, 3).

In a focused, applied approach specifically crafted for business leaders, Hansen's key aims were to develop

- Curiosity about business problems

- Sensitivity to people in business organizations

- Intellectual and emotional discipline, through the hard, continuing search for facts and the willingness to lose rather than compromise the rules of the game

- A sense of responsibility that goes beyond self

all in the context of 'taking up the challenge' and not putting it off until another time as 'that time may never come' (Hansen 1970: 4). This latter observation points up the significance of time in seizing opportunities, although any strategy must always be informed by the facts of a situation, the search for which is ongoing. In other words, the business leader must be a continuous learner, assimilating relevant information and discarding that which is not. This searching, screening and assimilation will be directed and influenced by prior knowledge and experience that creates the 'absorptive capacity' (Cohen and Levinthal 1990) of an individual in the learning process. As such, a general learning experience may be appropriated specifically and uniquely, depending on individual history.

We have earlier noted how the individual experience and prior knowledge of the founder members of Catering & Allied enabled the creation of a unique market niche: the provision of top quality restaurant facilities in the workplace, destroying the traditional canteen culture at a stroke. Such creative processes do not only generate demand, however, they also drive up expectations. This means that the context of service delivery is constantly evolving, through the reciprocal dynamic between customer and provider. One factor of especial significance within this wider context is that of culture, and it is from this perspective that the following section addresses the continuous learning experience of Catering & Allied through proactive membership of the erstwhile Industrial Catering Association (ICA) that, under the national chairmanship of Verstringhe, in 1989 affiliated to the European Catering Association (ECA) and changed its name to ECA (Great Britain).

From ICA to ECA – an evolving context for learning

The ICA was founded following an inaugural meeting of 120 industrial caterers on 3 December 1937 during the Hotel, Restaurant and Catering Exhibition at Olympia. The resolution was moved that an association of industrial caterers be formed and a provisional committee appointed to draft objectives and a constitution, with the *Caterer and Hotelkeeper* trade journal to be adopted as the nascent association's official organ. The main objective of the ICA, whose committee first met formally on 2 January 1938, was to provide industrial catering managers with a forum for debate and a status commensurate with their position within the catering industry.

With the outbreak of World War II and the consequent rationing of foodstuffs, the period 1939-1945 saw the government introduction of canteens at work, to ensure that war workers benefited from a meal while on duty. British Restaurants developed alongside this initiative, to serve the wider community as a whole, whilst many voluntary organizations were also engaged in providing meals to members of the armed forces and other public sector personnel. Experience by members of the fledgling ICA was thereby rapidly gained, both in feeding large numbers of people and improving on basic foodstuffs in a period of austerity encapsulated in such recipes as Woolton Pie, 'a stew of root vegetables covered in an unidentifiable white sauce, the whole surmounted in mashed potato' (Barwood 1994). It was during this time that the advantages of corporate catering were perhaps fully recognized and, as discussed in Chapters One and Two of this book, the sustained dynamic created for the development of the multi-national, multi-billion pound industry contract catering has become today.

On 21 April 1983, the decision was taken to incorporate the ICA as a company limited by guarantee, with the following principal aims and objectives:

- To raise the standards of industrial, institutional and staff catering generally

- To promote the interchange of knowledge, information and ideas on all matters of general interest to those engaged in industrial and allied organizations

- To lay down standards of conduct and performance, and to give guidance to members on the observance of professional conduct

- To encourage training, education, and general advancement of knowledge

- To promote by means of scholarships, prizes, cups, medals and other awards, competitions and other projects connected with the association and the industry

- To liaise with government departments, education authorities, training boards, and other similar bodies

Prominent among these from the point of view of Verstringhe, who was elected national chairman of the ICA for the period 1989-1991, was the interchange and advancement of knowledge in the context of professional training and development. He has consistently sought to activate the links between business education and the catering industry and it was, in fact, his involvement in creating opportunities for learning that led him into the ICA. Catering & Allied participated in the student sponsorship scheme initiated in the mid 1980s by Brian Watts of the Bank of England, which grew to encompass several city of London companies and led in 1987 to Mr Watts receiving the prestigious Catey Award for Industrial Caterer of the Year, through which he was 'honoured for his generosity in helping colleagues and for piloting within his company a student sponsorship scheme which worked so well he brought in other industrial caterers to widen the programme' (*Caterer & Hotelkeeper*, 1 February 1990: 73). The aim of the scheme was to give opportunities to young catering professionals who lacked the financial means to go to college and simultaneously to promote to students and their lecturers the career advantages offered by the industrial catering sector. The initiative flourished to such an extent that it threatened to overwhelm sponsoring companies and the decision was taken, under the chairmanship of Verstringhe, to incorporate the scheme into the ICA (cf *Hospitality*, April 1994).

Perhaps Verstringhe's most significant contribution to the ICA during this time, however, was through his initiative to affiliate with the ECA in anticipation of Europe 1992.

At an extraordinary general meeting of the ICA, held on 21 October 1989, the results of a postal ballot on three resolutions previously circulated to the membership were reported. These resolutions – all of which were passed, each having received a favourable vote of 75% minimum as required by the rules of the Association - were as follows:

a) that the Industrial Catering Association change its name to the European Catering Association (GB)

b) that the Association become affiliated to the ECA

c) that action be taken by the board of management to secure the title 'The Industrial Catering Association'

All three were the initiative of Verstringhe as national chairman of the ICA who, in his speech at the annual conference in

November 1989, announced the results and elucidated the thinking behind the development. In anticipation of the European Community - the economic community of twelve European nations (Belgium, Denmark, France, Germany, Greece, Republic of Ireland, Italy, Luxembourg, the Netherlands, Portugal, Spain, and the UK) that also shared certain social and political objectives – the theme of the conference was 'Into Europe – 1992 and beyond', and Verstringhe noted the 'unique opportunity' now afforded to the Association 'because we represent in our segment of the industry (industrial catering) both employer and employee, direct caterers and catering contractors, and as such we can speak with one voice. This should give us a unique opportunity to lobby Brussels. It sets us apart from other Associations that could be seen to be partisan in their interest'.

This may be seen to encapsulate the musketeering philosophy that informed Verstringhe in all his business activities, realizing and building on the inherent strengths in the 'all for one and one for all' approach that assigns equal voice and value to all involved in the pursuit of a common aim. The significance of the affiliation of the ICA to ECA International was endorsed by an editorial in the *Caterer & Hotelkeeper* of 16 November 1989: 9 describing it as 'an important move' with the potential to 'raise the political profile of the British catering sector in Europe'. The industry also recognized the importance of this development on a more personal level when awarding Verstringhe the 1989 Catey Industrial Caterer of the Year. He was the first contract caterer to receive it, and was described as 'working tirelessly in his continuing endeavour to raise the standard and profile of the sector as a founder member of the HCIMA, a member of the BHRCA's industrial committee, and a leading light in the ICA' (*Caterer & Hotelkeeper*, 1 February 1990: 73). In 1991, following his term as national chairman of the ICA/ECA (GB), Verstringhe was elected president of ECA International, a post he held for the next seven years. Since 1998, he has been honorary president of the Association.

The ECA itself was founded in Copenhagen in May 1964 to establish a forum for professionals within direct and contract catering, suppliers and consultancies, with the aim of protecting, promoting and representing the interests of the

European catering industry. Its membership is drawn from 12 European countries, and also the USA; the Society for Foodservice Management (SFM) based in Kentucky became involved with ECA proceedings, specifically the annual student competition and student exchanges, during the presidency of Verstringhe, the idea of forming an alliance with American colleagues in the industry being initially discussed at the 1991 ECA annual conference. It was also at this conference, held at Louvain in Belgium, that the decision was taken to start an annual student competition, in recognition of the importance of creating a much better awareness of the opportunities afforded by the industry to young people. The first of these competitions was successfully held in 1992, in Budapest.

The ECA International Student of the Year Competition and Conference

The concept of an International Student of the Year Competition and Conference running in mutual association was informed by the objective of creating a forum for tutors, students, caterers, suppliers and consultants to facilitate network communications and learning, whilst heightening student awareness of the opportunities that exist in the contract catering sector of the hospitality industry.

The concept informing the ECA International competition grew from the idea of Catermind, a Student of the Year national competition that was held annually in the UK and ran for 20 years. The competition was based on the television quiz show 'Mastermind' and, from 1977, featured the host of the latter, Magnus Magnusson, conducting the London finals. Sheila Mitchell, current President of ECA (GB) and recipient of the 1986 Catey Industrial Caterer of the Year for, *inter alia*, 'her work with the Industrial Catering Association and her dedication to the annual and evergrowing student competition Catermind' (*Caterer & Hotelkeeper*, 1 February 1990), was responsible with Harry Andrews for running the competition, which was fostered in the West London branch of the ICA to promote contact with all the catering colleges and students throughout the UK. The competition began in 1974 with one heat between West London colleges and progressed until 1994, with the participation of 206 catering colleges in 14 heats throughout

Northern Ireland, Scotland, Wales and England.

Following the affiliation of the ICA with the ECA, it was decided by the board of ECA International under the presidency of Jack Koppels to hold trial competitions in Sweden, Holland and Belgium, organized respectively by Hjördis Frostenson, then responsible for education and training within ECA International, Peter van Wielink and Ferenc Veerman, and Dirk Lemaitre. In creating and developing the ideas for the competition as well as negotiating the challenges posed by a multilingual event, their contribution was key; the trial contests proved very successful and, as a result, the initiative was taken to hold a final between Belgium and Holland. The enthusiasm generated by the venture was such that the decision was taken at the 1991 ECA conference in Louvain to hold a full European competition, the first of which took place in 1992 at the conference in Budapest. Six countries participated, since which time the competition has doubled in size; in 2002, teams were fielded by 12 countries including the USA, which first competed in 1995. The competition involves teams of two students in a theory based, multiple choice quiz, in which each of 50 questions must be answered within 7 seconds, and a five minute 'Folkloristic' presentation designed to convey an understanding of the customs and culture as well as traditional food and/or drink of the team's country.

The annual conference and competition is organized within the ECA Secretariat and, from 1992-2001, was the particular responsibility of Mair Davison, personal assistant to Verstringhe and a member of ICA/ECA (GB) since 1989. In the ten years since the inception of the competition, Davison has established a close working relationship with Robert Perry, senior lecturer in Food Studies at the Ealing School of Hospitality, Tourism and Leisure within Thames Valley University, who sets the multiple choice questions and, since 1995, has been the student co-ordinator, Davison being the competition organizer. The questions themselves cover a range of topics, from alcoholic and non-alcoholic beverages, commodities, hygiene and nutrition through to health and safety, culinary terms, service and basic calculations, and are updated on an annual basis.

Perry and Davison describe their partnership as a 'team of two', constituting a learning process in which the competition proceedings and questions are reviewed in a continuously evolving context, with due regard to cultural sensibilities. Member countries take turns in staging the event, with the student information pack and conference brochure circulated beforehand traditionally including detail on the history and culture of the host city and its environs that will form the basis of some of the multiple choice questions. In respect of language, as part of the competition planning process the questions are submitted by Davison to a centralized translation facility which creates a book of questions in the language of each team, one question to a page, that the teams can consult as each question is read aloud in English by the question master. Likewise, in the Folkloristic section, EFL teams can choose to make their presentations in their native language although one minute of the five minute presentation must be given in English; conversely, in English speaking countries, one minute of the presentation must be given in one other European language.

The approach of the competition and conference is designed to promote cultural integration and understanding in a learning context, as well as create opportunities for the networking that constitutes a significant dynamic in hospitality. In particular, Davison and Perry note the enduring networks and contacts developed by students despite their initial meeting in a competitive environment; this is a significant point as the students who enter are drawn from the wider catering context, not just from within contract catering, and the relationships they forge may be seen as a microcosm of the ECA in enhancing, integrating and disseminating a range of competencies across various areas of the industry as a whole.

ECARUS

A core aim of the ECA is to achieve business excellence through education, benchmarking and best practice, creating opportunities for individual and organizational development and progress in an increasingly dynamic, international industry. The Association is particularly concerned that growing skill shortages in smaller catering organizations is putting at risk job creation, career advancement and economic growth, and is thus committed to the initial education and advancement of young people studying catering, a commitment that, as noted above, led initially to the annual student competition. It also recognizes the importance of continuing professional development of staff already employed (Battersby 1998) and these dual emphases on learning are reflected in the ECARUS initiative, a programme for continuing professional development established in 1996 to

a) define professional training criteria that are valid throughout the whole of Europe and take into account the rapid evolution of this sector of activity

b) develop training programmes that are modular and progressive, can be accessed via the internet and distributed by a European network of teaching establishments

c) achieve recognition of the training provided, the latter being supported by means of an aptitude certificate that provides access to all ECA member countries.

The pursuit of these objectives has realized an international network of partnerships within the food and catering industries, including the Hotel and Catering International Management Association (HCIMA); the European Foundation for the Accreditation of Hotel Schools (EFAH); the Food Service Consultants Society International (FCSI Europe); the European Federation of Contract Catering Organisations (FERCO); the Irish State Agency for Tourism Training (CERT); the Savoy Educational Trust and the Fondation Nestlé Pro-Gastronomia.

The ECARUS programme has been developed under the guidance and leadership of David Battersby, since 1990 the managing director of Hospitality and Leisure Manpower (to where the ECA secretariat was transferred in 2001) and previously director of training for the Hotel and Catering Training Board. He was created OBE in the Queen's 1998 New Year's Honours List for services to education and training in the tourism and hospitality industry. In respect of individual learning, the four programmes presented in the guide for 2002 include supervisory development, operational management, business management and strategic management, all of which are designed to contribute to a recognized award; respectively, an HCIMA Certificate, HNC and NVQ/SVQ; an HCIMA Diploma, HND and NVQ/SVQ; a TVU BA Degree in Hospitality Management; and, in respect of three levels of strategic management, to an Oxford Brookes Certificate or Diploma in Management (Hospitality) and, ultimately, an Oxford Brookes MBA (Hospitality). In this way, the learning offered can accommodate all those who wish to progress within the industry, whatever their individual interest and stage of development.

For those who do not fulfil the entry requirements for their chosen programme, Accreditation of Prior Learning (APL) is a process that gives credit for learning by experience in the workplace and previous education or training, with further encouragement offered across all programmes by the emphasis on mentor support in the workplace and best practice benchmarking. Partnership endorsement of the scheme is evidenced, *inter alia*, by the offer, current at the time of writing, of £250 funding by the Savoy Educational Trust to any learner who registers with the Hospitality Learning Network through ECARUS. Current initiatives of the ECA include development of the Network to cover action planning, using computer based assessments of skill needs and the production of a learning action plan for both establishments and individual employees, the opening of the ECARUS scheme to other European countries, and the recognition of achievement through the ECA Catering Passport in partnership with ECTIS.

References

Argyris, C (2000). *Flawed advice and the management trap*. Oxford: OUP

Argyris, C and D A Schön (1978). *Organizational learning: A theory of action perspective*. Reading, MA: Addison-Wesley

Barwood, R (1994). 'The Association'. Unpublished ms, 7 April.

Battersby, D (1998). 'ECARUS update report'. In ECA Newsletter, Summer Edition

Caterer & Hotelkeeper, 1 February 1990

Caterer & Hotelkeeper, 16 November 1989

Child, J (2001). 'Learning through strategic alliances'. In M Dierkes, A B Antal, J Child and I Nonaka (eds) *Handbook of organizational learning and knowledge*. Oxford: OUP, 657-680

Child, J and S J Heavens (2001). 'The social constitution of organizations and its implications for organizational learning'. In M Dierkes, A B Antal, J Child and I Nonaka (eds) *Handbook of organizational learning and knowledge*. Oxford: OUP, 308-326

Cohen, W M and D A Levinthal (1990). 'Absorptive capacity: A new perspective on learning and innovation'. *Administrative Science Quarterly*, 35: 128-52

Corrigan, P (1999) *Shakespeare on management: Leadership lessons for today's managers*. London: Kogan Page

Cyert, R M and J G March (1992). *A behavioral theory of the firm*. 2nd edition. Oxford: Blackwell

Dierkes, M, A B Antal, J Child and I Nonaka (eds) (2001). *Handbook of Organizational Learning and Knowledge*, Oxford: Oxford University Press

Farkas, C, P de Backer and A Sheppard (1995). *Maximum leadership*. London: Orion

Garvin, D A (1993). 'Building a learning organization'. *Harvard Business Review*, 71/4: 78-91

Grinyer, P H, D G Mayes and P McKiernan (1988). *Sharpbenders*. Oxford: Blackwell

Hamel, G (1991). 'Competition for competence and inter-partner learning within international strategic alliances'. *Strategic Management Journal*, 12 (Summer special issue): 83-103

Handy, C (1990). *Inside organizations*. London: Penguin

Hansen, H L (1970). 'The aims of business education'. Reprinted from *Harvard Business School Bulletin*, 46/6

Huber, G P (1991). 'Organizational learning: The contributing processes and the literatures'. *Organization Science*, 2/1: 88-115

Inkpen, A C (1996). 'Creating knowledge through collaboration'. *California Management Review*, 39/1: 123-140

Kanter, R M (1989) *When giants learn to dance*. New York: Simon and Schuster

Kim, D H (1993). 'The link between individual and organizational learning'. *Sloan Management Review*, 35/1: 37-50

Kirton, M J (1994). 'A theory of cognitive style'. In M Kirton (ed) *Adaptors and innovators: Styles of creativity and problem solving*. London: Routledge, 1-33

Lindholm, N (1997). 'Learning Processes in International Joint Ventures in China'. *Advances in Chinese Industrial Studies*, 5: 139-154.

Lipparini, A and L Fratocchi (1999). 'The capabilities of the transnational firm: Accessing knowledge and leveraging inter-firm relationships'. *European Management Journal*, 17/6: 655-667

Lyles, M A (2001). 'Organizational learning in international joint ventures: The case of Hungary'. In M Dierkes, A B Antal, J Child and I Nonaka (eds) *Handbook of organizational learning and knowledge*. Oxford: OUP, 681-698

Nonaka, I and H Takeuchi (1995). *The knowledge creating company*. Oxford: OUP

Nonaka, I, R Toyama and P Byosière (2001). 'A theory of organizational knowledge creation: Understanding the dynamic process of creating knowledge'. In M Dierkes, A B Antal, J Child and I Nonaka (eds) *Handbook of organizational learning and knowledge*. Oxford: OUP, 491-517

Pavitt, K (1991). 'Key characteristics of the large innovating firm'. *British Journal of Management*, 2/1: 41-50

Peters, T J and R H Waterman Jr (1982). *In search of excellence*. New York: Harper & Row

Powell, W.W., Koput, K.W. and Smith-Doerr, L. (1996) 'Interorganizational Collaboration and the Locus of Innovation: Networks of Learning in Biotechnology'. *Administrative Science Quarterly*, 41: 116-145.

Sadler, P (2001). 'Leadership and organizational learning'. In M Dierkes, A B Antal, J Child and I Nonaka (eds) *Handbook of organizational learning and knowledge*. Oxford: OUP, 415-427

Selznick, P (1957). *Leadership in administration: A sociological interpretation*. New York: Harper & Row

Senge, P (1990). 'The leader's new work: Building learning organizations'. *Sloan Management Review*, 32/1: 7-23

Sivula, P, F A J van den Bosch and T Elfring (1997). 'Competence building by incorporating clients into the development of a business service firm's knowledge base'. In R Sanchez and A Heene (eds) *Strategic learning and knowledge management*. Chichester: John Wiley, 121-137

Stata, R (1989). 'Organizational learning – the key to management innovation'. *Sloan Management Review*, 30/3: 63-73

Sutton, A (1994). 'A man who never stops learning'. *Hospitality*, April: 16-17

Von Krogh, G, K Ichijo and I Nonaka (2000). *Enabling knowledge creation*. Oxford: OUP

Chapter Eight

Insights and Implications

The organizational experiences discussed in this study stemmed essentially from two questions that may be seen to have significance for business in general, not just at start up but throughout the life of an organization: What can we offer that will attract, and even addict, clients (cf Ridderstråle and Nordström 2002)? What can we offer that will attract people to work with us? In a service company, the answers particularly inhere in customer and personnel relations and the structures and processes that encourage and facilitate these both within and across organizational boundaries. The following sections consider some of these wider organizational issues through the experiences of Catering & Allied in its sector.

A strategy for service

Strategy and its associated concept of leadership (cf Normann 1991) have been increasingly debated in the literature yet, as Leavy and Wilson (1994: 1) point out, 'we still seem to be a long way from fully understanding these two concepts and how they are inter-related'. This observation offers a useful and integrative perspective on the issues raised in the previous chapters. As earlier discussed, strategy (Chapter Two) includes the organizational structures and processes implicit within and fundamental to competitive initiatives such as client relations (Chapter Four), personnel development (Chapter Five), partnerships and alliances (Chapter Six), whilst the concept of leadership evokes themes of entrepreneurship, management and learning (Chapters Three and Seven). As organizational phenomena, however, none of these are mutually exclusive, and it is clear from earlier discussions that issues of leadership both inform, and are informed by, the strategic positioning of an organization in its market as illustrated by the differentiation focus (Porter 1985, 1998) of Catering & Allied. The cyclical dynamic thus created is fundamental to organizational evolution.

The strategy of the Catering & Allied founders was deceptively simple and innovative; to take their existing competencies and apply them in a unique context (cf Bolton 1993). Thus, as hoteliers/restaurateurs, they mobilized their skills to transform the canteen culture of industrial catering in a 'total commitment to client satisfaction – no ifs, no buts'. This differentiation focus had two main elements: geographical focus, and customer focus. In respect of the former, the decision by the London company to keep the area of operation within a 35 mile radius of the City impacted on the latter, in ensuring that top management remained accessible both to clients and unit teams. This geographical 'tightness' was mirrored in the organizational structure, which limited the responsibility of each operations manager to 20 units, with an on-site manager for each. The consensus, based on previous experience, was that above this level the accessibility and responsiveness of operations management to client and unit manager/team need would be compromised.

Holland Catering also operated on the basis of 20 units per account manager, with the units in close proximity to one another. As a result of their burgeoning contract with Shell, however, and Shell's desire to keep the same account manager, the position of group manager was eventually introduced to enable a continuing, dedicated service over four geographically spread units. There are now nine group managers within Holland Catering, yielding an interesting illustration of the structural evolution of the company through ongoing client relations whilst also pointing up Koops' emphasis on maintaining continuity in these relationships. His main concern is 'how do we keep our clients', although this does not necessarily mean keeping the same manager *in situ*. He notes that, although continuity of personnel is good for a certain length of time, change is also important. When, for example, the manager of their units was in line for promotion after four or five years, Shell became concerned at this perceived removal of 'their' manager. Loyalties were becoming blurred and, from the perspective of Holland Catering, removing this manager through promotion was a good thing for both the individual and the client.

Flexibility within a structural framework is key. The link-manning approach to service delivery (Chapter Five) – an organizational innovation again informed by the client relationship, with CDP in London – epitomizes this. The system throws into relief, not simply the transfer of both tacit and explicit knowledge between team members (cf Nonaka and Takeuchi 1995) but the way in which organizational structure and process facilitate the application and recontextualization of such knowledge by individuals in unique ways, thereby enabling innovation and knowledge creation. The rotation of personnel through a variety of functions exhibits elements of entrepreneurship including leadership, management and learning with, for example, the drawing up and implementation of a formal system and schedule of operation covering the routine tasks to be fulfilled (management), consequent upskilling through knowledge transfer (learning) and leadership (which involves not only direction but active participation in an initiative, and may be shared among a number of individuals).

The creative, customized approach to client service delivery attracted personnel to work with the company. Don Davenport notes:

> Catering & Allied positioned themselves – a little bit Continental in some ways; a little bit different in their offer, compared with other people; they attracted some people that were far more entrepreneurial ... they came up with lots of good, innovative designs and offers to the clients.

Although customer focus is increasingly recognized as key in successful business strategies today (cf Montgomery and Webster 1997), when Verstringhe, Cuthbert and Koops started out in 1975 their philosophy was radical, especially when applied to a customer base in which expectation was traditionally encapsulated in 'music hall jokes' about 'stodgy foods and urn flavoured tea' (New 1957). Thus, increasing client expectation was an integral part of winning business although, as noted in the Ford case study in Chapter Four, there were exceptions to this rule. As a niche player at the top end of the market, with a focus on quality, product and service, Catering & Allied learned through their work with Ford that quality is ultimately context dependent and inheres in meeting customer desire which, by its very nature, is highly personal and subjective. It can, for example, inhere in the act of offering choice in accordance with previous expectation, irrespective of what that choice might actually be.

Successful implementation of the dual philosophy of 'total commitment' to the client and 'people working with not for' also led to the development of Catering & Allied's portfolio of services; for example, the provision of reception services at Deutsche Bank and global conferencing facilities for Smith Kline Beecham. Each exemplifies, as do the link manning scheme for CDP and the introduction of a group manager for Shell in Holland, an initiative that became part of the company repertoire, informed by a specific customer need and subsequently translated into other areas of its business.

Entrepreneurship

(i) Identity

Perhaps the most striking examples of the issues raised by the processes of entrepreneurship are offered by the experiences of the London company in its bid to grow whilst staying small. In the mid 1980s, the business was divided into two 'houses', Carlton and Metropole, with Robert Lawson and Peter Price, then Ann Cripps, as respective managing directors. The initiative, which was based on the principles and concepts of the public school system and informed by the perception that 50 units was the maximum for top management in respect of personal attention and efficiency at unit level (cf *What's Cooking*, Issue No 4, 1988), did not last long. Verstringhe recalls that it created some confusion and unnecessary competition, ultimately proving a divisive factor, and is straightforward about the action taken when it was perceived that the concept was not working. 'It was affecting team spirit – so we ditched it'.

He believes that the main problem inhered in the creation of two distinct identities, such that the overall identity of Catering & Allied London was undermined. This raises a significant issue, as identity is clearly integral to both the perception of an organization from within and by others in the market place. It may also be seen to have been a contributory factor in the ultimately abortive Chiltern experiment discussed in Chapter Two. Its MD, Nigel Anker, felt the company to be peripheral, 'just one spoke of a hub' that was circumscribed by the wider,

London organization. As an individual, he perceived the venture to have been successful, enabling him to gain valuable experience with the 'luxury of a huge safety net', although from the point of view of Catering & Allied, it had not proved viable for the intended purpose of securing its long term future.

In a wider context, the issue of organizational identity has also proved significant; for example, Holland Catering Specialisten kept its name after takeover and has seen the company succession secured following the retirement in 2002 of Jop Koops, with Gosse Visser as CEO, Martin van den Heuvel as financial director and Bert Pilaszek - who joined the company in its early days from Sutcliffe Nederland - responsible for marketing and sales. This scenario reflects the 'internally grown' management philosophy of Koops within International as a whole; for example, Visser, a graduate of the Hague Hotelschool, commenced his career with the London company in order to familiarize himself with the culture and core philosophies of Catering & Allied. After a period as manager of Air Products, he returned to The Netherlands, progressing through Holland Catering to the position of director. At this point, he returned to London for two years, as a director responsible for 50% of the London company. This initiative was agreed by both Visser and the founders, as part of the Catering & Allied International top management succession programme, in a context in which Holland Catering has both retained its identity and >97% of its business over time.

Likewise Compass, the world leader in food services, kept the brand names and identity of the companies operating in the different segments and niches of the market (i.e. Baxter & Platts, Eurest, Restaurant Associates etc) and promoted many of the senior management of its merged and acquired business, for example Don Davenport from Sutcliffe/Granada to MD of Eurest UK. In respect of Sodexho, although the takeover saw the departure of a number of senior management including Bill Toner as director and, as a direct result of its change of name from Gardner Merchant, Garry Hawkes as CEO, the company has retained the brand name of Directors Table in London and clearly identified other specialized segments of its business, for example Sodexho Prestige.

In marked contrast to all the above, however, Catering & Allied London has experienced a change of name and loss of identity with many of the senior management team, including the financial director, IT manager, and operations directors, leaving to seek opportunities elsewhere. Dan Wright, who was MD from October 1998 to July 2000 and subsequently MD of Eliance until his departure in May 2001, notes in particular how he identified with Verstringhe's belief in 'team involvement' and an 'inclusive, non-hierarchical approach' to business that informed the reputation of Catering & Allied as a 'fun' company to work with. Of particular note in this respect is Wright's invitation to participate in the HUB Initiative, chaired by Lord Newton of the Institute of Directors with Oonagh Mary Harpur as CEO, and his contribution, with reference to the success of Catering & Allied in this regard, to the panel's work on strategies for building a sustainable business reputation and the core purposes and values that inform this. Post 2000, however, an increasing concern of Wright's was the London company's loss of identity, which he contrasts with the example of Compass for whom he previously consulted. He notes in particular that company's 'focused strategy of branding and segmentation' which ensures that established niche businesses retain their identities and reputational advantage.

In respect of Catering & Allied International, although Holland Catering has retained its identity - and its business - the strategy in respect of the London company has ultimately led to market perception of a niche opportunity being created for competitors: in a recent article in the *Caterer & Hotelkeeper* (Baker 2002) Alan Walker, the managing director of Eaton Group, 'the largest independent contract caterer in the city of London', observes that

> There is a general move by clients away from the large companies, and we are well positioned to be the successor to replace former leading independents such as Catering & Allied or High Table.

(ii) From intrapreneur to entrepreneur

On an individual basis, there are interesting parallels in the route taken by Verstringhe within Sutcliffe and John Houston,

London MD from 1983 to 1997, within Catering & Allied. Chapter Three describes the evolution of the former from intrapreneur to entrepreneur, following a prescribed career path that was enhanced by the mentoring relationship he enjoyed first with Mickie O'Brien and subsequently Harry Hansen, and ultimately progressing to the creation with his co-founders of a new direction which others then could follow in a mentoring context in which, as noted above, management could be internally grown. Koops observes that integral to competitive advantage is the willingness to 'take it on your own neck'. This expresses the risk element of entrepreneurship as opposed to the 'safety net' of intrapreneurship, whilst also conveying a faith in the individual that will translate into the continuous process of building trust and confidence within both the company and the client base.

John Houston began his career in hotel management with Trust House Hotels as an indentured trainee on their five year programme, rotating through kitchen, reception, bar and finally assistant manager functions. In 1969, he joined Sutcliffe West of England, progressing from area manager to director with responsibility for Bristol, the South West and Wales, moving after nine years to Grand Metropolitan as director of the northern area business of Midland Catering. After a spell in Mexico, first with Servicios Grand Metropolitan and then, briefly, with a company brewing Mexican beer, he returned to England. and, having maintained good relations with Grand Metropolitan, rejoined the organization as director of their Berni Inns division. He moved to Catering & Allied as MD of the London company in 1983, an opportunity created by the decision of Kit Cuthbert to scale down to a three day week. He found Verstringhe to be a 'strong personality', a 'passionate' figure with 'phenomenal strength' whose ownership of the business clearly impacted on the style and approach of the company. Although he shared the vision of Catering & Allied, not least because of the values he had imbibed at Sutcliffe, Houston ultimately found – as Verstringhe himself had in 1975 – that his own way forward ultimately lay in creating his own niche in the market; in other words, moving from intrapreneur to entrepreneur.

In 1997, Houston left Catering & Allied and, after a short period in consultancy, founded his own contract catering company, Houston & Church, with an initial personal investment of £10,000. In respect of organizational identity and market perception, it is interesting to note that there was no partner 'Church': 'Houston did not want to be seen as a one-man band and thought that the name Church sounded respectable' (Baker 2001). Starting from scratch, with an initial focus on in-house cafés/delicatessens and expansion into staff restaurants over time, the company turned over £1.5m in its first year of trading and has grown consistently ever since, achieving just under £8m turnover on 23 units by end 2001 (*Caterer & Hotelkeeper*, 16 January 2002). As part of its wider development programme, the company entered into a strategic alliance with Wilson Storey Halliday (WSH) in May 2001 in order to benefit from back-office support including accounting, personnel, health and safety, IT support and purchasing (cf *Caterer & Hotelkeeper*, 24 May 2001), which in turn informed the underlying objective to provide a customized, personalized service. In January 2002, in further pursuit of the client led philosophy, a new MD appointment was made with Houston moving to the role of chairman. This new position was created 'in an attempt to keep regular personal contact with customers as the company grows' (*Caterer & Hotelkeeper*, 16 January 2002), an emphasis on client relations and service the provenance of which may be traced back through Catering & Allied, Sutcliffe Catering and ultimately the post-war partnership between Jack Bateman and John Sutcliffe within Factory Canteens.

(iii) The wider context

Organizational growth within the food services industry is characterized by two major features: merger and acquisition and the exiting of individuals from larger companies to form new organizations that, if successful, become integral to this wider process. A particularly striking example of this is Compass, whose merger with Granada may be seen ultimately to rehearse the original partnership between Jack Bateman and John Sutcliffe over 50 years before. This ended when the latter broke away, first trading as Factory Canteens (West of England) and subsequently founding Sutcliffe Catering, which was ultimately taken over by Granada (*see* Chapter Two). Meanwhile, the latter founded Batemans, which was ultimately taken over by Grand Metropolitan/Compass (*see* Chapter One). With the demerger of Compass from Granada, history may be seen to have come full circle.

Likewise, this study of Catering & Allied reflects the cyclical dynamic of breakaway start up through to merger and eventual acquisition, with the pattern continuing through, for example, the subsequent departure of two Avenance directors, Andrew Wilson and Caroline Vale, to form a new contract catering company (Wilson Vale) focusing on business and industry and the independent schools sector in an area covering north London to Leeds (*Caterer & Hotelkeeper*, 13 December 2001). Another eponymous business, Wilson Storey, exhibits both characteristics of organizational growth but as an acquirer; founded by Keith Wilson and Alastair Storey, previously financial director and CEO of Granada, the company subsequently took over Halliday Catering to become WSH Group which, as noted above, has since entered into a strategic alliance with Houston & Church. A further, very recent example of individual start-up is that of Mark Philpott, previously MD of Director's Table, and Clive Hetherington, the FD of Eaton Group and, before this, head of accounts within Catering & Allied; their focus will be City business and industry (*Caterer & Hotelkeeper*, 1 August 2002. Their move represents the first stage of entrepreneurial development, significant in which is the differentiation focus, or niche positioning, that will set the new organization apart from its competitors.

Of particular note in respect of entrepreneurial activity is William Baxter, who co-founded his first company with Robert Platts in October 1987. They became 'great pals' through fly fishing, having first met through their work within Sutcliffe, and started their company with an initial investment of £15,000 each plus a £40,000 bank loan. Focusing on the corporate head office sector of the market, they won their first contract six months after start-up and gradually built their business over nine and a half years to achieve turnover of £35m. In 1997, Baxter & Platts was acquired by Granada for £15m (£16.5m after earn out) and, through the merger/demerger with Compass, has ultimately become part of the latter organization. Baxter notes that the offer itself prompted the sale although Platts had been suffering some health problems and was able to retire, since when he has recovered 'excellent' health. In the meantime, Baxter, having remained as executive chairman of Baxter & Platts for two and a half years and then taken a six month break, was able to re-enter the market. The terms of the sale of their company had included a non-competition clause, prohibiting ownership by either Baxter or Platts of more than 3% of a catering company for three years, but now Baxter was able to start again, which he did in May 2000 with Mike Smith. Again focusing on the corporate head office sector – and, intriguingly, in apparent competition with himself, the Baxter & Platts name having been retained by Compass - BaxterSmith has built to a current turnover of £16m on 31 contracts.

The way ahead

The market still remains open and buoyant for all those who, in the words of Baxter, Koops, and Verstringhe, really enjoy the industry and love to give service. It is true that the nature of contract catering is changing, with clients moving away from the traditional philanthropy of subsidized staff feeding and increasingly seeking to make a profit, but this opens out new possibilities for contractors. For example, the Café Plus experiment by Catering & Allied, introduced in the early 1990s as a temporary measure at Coopers & Lybrand whilst the staff restaurant was refurbished, proved so popular that it was retained. Subsequently, UBS Warburg approached Catering & Allied to install a similar facility in their premises as, though unsubsidized, it could still compete on price with the High Street. This was the first experience by Catering & Allied of a client making a profit on staff feeding. The Café Plus concept was adopted by Holland Catering and developed, in a multi-tenancy location, to accommodate commercial as well as client business, the in-house facility also opening out onto the street. Prices were geared to the High Street, with the electronic credit cards of in-house customers being programmed to give a discount on purchases. Generally, the emphasis on retail catering within the food services industry is increasing with the phasing out of cost plus contracts and the need for contractors to become more commercial as they assume the risk of an operation. It is encouraging diversification in facilities and services, with branding and marketing as key, although customer relations remain fundamental to the whole.

The desire for personal service remains paramount, however, as evidenced by the continuing market for independent niche players whose focus enables the attention to detail and flexibility inherent in the customized approach. As Verstringhe observes, in the words of his mentor Hansen, business is fundamentally about 'finding a creative response to challenges' and imagining what should be, rather than accepting what is possible. It is a philosophy that remains as pertinent for entrepreneurs today as it was for Catering & Allied over 25 years ago.

References

Baker, J (2002). 'Eaton out'. *Caterer & Hotelkeeper*, 20 June: 34-35

Baker, J (2001). 'Independent paths'. *Caterer & Hotelkeeper*, 6 September: 33-34

Baxter, W. *Personal interview*, August 2002

Bolton, M K (1993). 'Organizational innovation and substandard performance: When is necessity the mother of innovation?'. *Organization Science*, 4: 57-75

Caterer & Hotelkeeper, 1 August 2002

Caterer & Hotelkeeper, 16 January 2002

Caterer & Hotelkeeper, 13 December 2001

Caterer & Hotelkeeper, 24 May 2001

Houston, J. *Personal interview*, January 2002

Leavy, B and D Wilson (1994). *Strategy and leadership*. London: Routledge

Montgomery, D B and F E Webster Jr (1997). 'Marketing's interfunctional interfaces: The MSI workshop on management of corporate fault zones'. *Journal of Market Focused Management*, 2: 7-26

New, J G (1957). *Office and works catering*. London: Business Publications

Nonaka, I and H Takeuchi (1995). *The knowledge creating company*. Oxford: OUP

Normann, R (1991). *Service management: Strategy and leadership in service business*. Chichester: John Wiley

Porter, M E (1985, 1998). *Competitive advantage*. New York: The Free Press

Ridderstråle, J and K Nordström (2002). *Funky business*. 2nd edition. London: Prentice Hall

What's Cooking, Issue No 4, 1988

EPILOGUE

In the 1960s there was much controversy in Britain about the value of a Harvard style advanced management programme based on the case teaching method. In having been an MBA student of Professor Harry Hansen at Harvard and as the chairman of council and founder subscriber of the foundation for management education, I supported the initiative taken by Denys Scott of J Walter Thompson for the Harvard faculty to run a one-off six week course in the UK, which I sponsored in 1965. As a result of its success the AMPI Trust was established and over the next 20 years some 1000 senior executives took advantage of the teaching as well as academics and trade union officials to whom we offered a scholarship. Says Hansen:

> Business schools should impart more than technical competence, they should begin the education of architects of a new and better economic order. The challenge is a managerial one: the marshalling, deployment and use of resources so that man can live a better and safer life, and a more fulfilling one.

This book has built upon both the strength of the case study as well as the authors' broad knowledge of business management. As a pupil of Harry Hansen in 1972 and having been invited to succeed me as the chairman of the AMPI Trust in 1985, Marc Verstringhe has worked with Sally Heavens and Professor John Child of the Centre for International Business and Management at Cambridge University to write this book. He is an outstanding business entrepreneur, using modern methods and sharing with his staff and colleagues the fruits of his success. *Managing to Serve* explores the contribution of Catering & Allied in its sector and, through its focus on major management themes such as entrepreneurship, teamwork, relationship marketing and managing partnerships, offers valuable lessons for general business practice.

Dr John Bolton CBE DSC DL

INDEX

Honeywell Controls, 106-107
Hygiene Impact
(see Gardner, Derek)
MD Personnel Services
(MDPS) (see Duffay, Mike)
Ferro Design, 107
Hodge, Ron, 107-108
Lawson Software, 112-113, 117
Nutt, Chris, 107
Servequip (see Hodge, Ron)
Sharpe, Harry, 111
Stapleton, Fergus, 107
Sutcliffe Catering, 21, 33, 70, 158
    Acquired by Granada, 22
    Acquired by Stirling
    Guarantee Trust, 21 24
    Foundation of, 6
    History, 22-23, 24
    Philosophy, 23-24
    Sutcliffe Set Standards, 79
Sutcliffe, John, 6, 14, 22, 158
SV-Service, 119
Thomas, Frank, 52, 53
Toner, Bill, 155
Tremain, Mike (see also
    Ford Motor Company Limited),
    67-70
Trout, Digby, 28, 118, 119
Trust, 51, 93, 105-106
Trusthouse Forte, 13
Trust Houses Ltd
    Merger with Forte (Holdings) Ltd,
    12
University of Cambridge
    Centre for International Business
    and Management (CIBAM), 138
    Judge Insitute of Management, 138
van den Heuvel, Martin, 155
van Wielink, Peter, 145
Veerman, Ferenc, 145
Verstringhe, Marc (*passim*)

ICA/ECA initiative, 142-143
Industrial Caterer of the Year, 143
Mentor significance, 47, 48, 137, 157
Philosophy and values, 57, 58, 130, 143
Professional development, 21, 22-23, 46-49, 79, 119, 143
Shareholding in Catering & Allied, 52-55
Shareholding in Eurocater, 121
Visser, Gosse, 69, 155
Walker, Alan, 156
Watts, Brian, 142
Webb, Roland (see Midland Counties
    Industrial Catering Limited)
Wilson Storey Halliday
    (WSH Group), 39, 159
Wilson Vale, 159
Work organization, 24-25, 77-100
    Control, 98-99
    Decentralization, 92
    Link manning, 23, 34, 51, 66, 67, 92-93, 95-98, 99, 152
    Modular management system, 61, 62, 80, 89-91, 99, 152
    Teamwork, 94-95, 98
Wright, Dan, 69, 156